Pagan Portals
# Artemis

## Goddess of the Wild Hunt & Sovereign Heart

Irisanya Moon

**MOON
BOOKS**
Winchester, UK
Washington, USA

JOHN HUNT PUBLISHING

First published by Moon Books, 2024
Moon Books is an imprint of John Hunt Publishing Ltd., No. 3 East Street, Alresford
Hampshire SO24 9EE, UK
office@jhpbooks.net
www.johnhuntpublishing.com
www.moon-books.net

For distributor details and how to order please visit the 'Ordering' section on our website.

Text copyright: Irisanya Moon 2023

ISBN: 978 1 80341 321 1
978 1 80341 322 8 (ebook)
Library of Congress Control Number: 2023930428

A CIP catalogue record for this book is available from the British Library.

Design: Lapiz Digital Services

UK: Printed and bound by CPI Group (UK) Ltd, Croydon, CR0 4YY
Printed in North America by CPI GPS partners

We operate a distinctive and ethical publishing philosophy in
all areas of our business, from our global network of authors to
production and worldwide distribution.

Pagan Portals
# Artemis

Goddess of the Wild Hunt &
Sovereign Heart

# Contents

Often pictured running in the woods, Artemis is a goddess unto Herself. She is wild, and She is the Wild. Through Her, we can learn about tapping back into our wildness, learning to care for our hearts, and returning to the places that we have been told to fear. Artemis' aim is always true, some say, and building a relationship with Her can help set the best direction for our own arrows.

# Acknowledgments

First, I want to thank my publisher, Moon Books, for their encouragement and feedback. I am a better writer for the ongoing collaboration. And to Trevor, thank you for your thoughtful notes and edits, as well as your patience as I continue to forget how to format things properly.

This book would not have been possible without the inspiration of a fateful witch camp back in 2016. While I will share how I met Artemis a long time ago, I really MET Her when I was at this camp. In the woods in Canada, I felt Her running by my side and traveling into my being like a spell. Like the spell we all created together. Because we are already magick.

And I thank my heart for its courage and its strength. I thank myself for reclaiming my own wild and embracing myself as possible, true, and strong. As with any wildness, it comes with complications and mistakes. But reclaiming myself has been worth it.

To a certain degree, this book hunted me until I started to write it. For that, I am honored and blessed.

# Author's Note

One of the things I want you, dear reader, to know before you move forward is that I trust you to take from this book what you will and want. Take what makes sense and what calls to your wild heart. No matter where you are in your spiritual journey and where you want to go, I encourage you to trust what feels good.

I do not believe my relationship with any godd is the right way. Just as when I see Artemis, I see a certain image, you may see another. You may know Her differently and perfectly, seeing Her through the eyes of your experience and your desire. Right now, offer yourself permission to honor what is true for you.

My goal with all of my books is to give you enough information to be excited to dive deeper and to build a relationship that works with you and the deity. And, if I'm being honest, I hope that this construction of connection will birth a better relationship with yourself and with others. All of this is connected, for me, anyway.

While you might be a person that wants to take notes and to do things 'right,' leave some space for magick and mystery. Leave some space for running wild in the woods with your thoughts and your dreams. Be willing to name and hold the arrows of your intentions before you launch them into the world. And be willing to shoot when you feel the timing is just right. Because it is. It might not result in what you imagined, but more often than not, it is better.

I believe Artemis is being called into these times, like a friend and a trusted ally. She can call us back to the wild hunt and claim our sovereignty (our ability to self-govern and be self-possessed). Artemis is not one of just play and delight, though She is that too, She is a being of action and alignment. She knows

Her values and acts on them. And even Artemis made mistakes that became stars in the sky. Remember that too.

These Pagan Portals books are meant to introduce readers to the godds and mysterious ones. For me, these books serve as a first meeting, a moment where you can get to know each other better. Where you can find common ground or find a spark that ignites a relationship.

Whether you spend a day or a lifetime with Artemis, I wish you well.

## Additional Notes

Before you continue reading, I want to let you know that I offer a complicated and potentially challenging description of Artemis. While there are stories of Her fierceness, they are often tempered and treated lightly. You may not have heard of some of the stories I share in this book.

Artemis is also cruel and unforgiving. She is powerful and feared. She has demanded sacrifices, and She has been described as having very strict ideas about virginity. These thoughts come primarily from research into translations of primary texts, which have been done primarily by men. To me, this requires analysis into what might have patriarchal influence and thus may not be telling the whole story. This is not to offset the harshness of some of the stories of Artemis, but I want to make this known before you continue reading.

She is a hunter, which can be softened by using 'huntress' to make it sound more romantic. Hunting's goal is death. Let us not forget that in the journey to know Her better. And while death is necessary to feed and can be necessary to protect, it is a harsh reality in a culture that fears death.

In addition, I recognize the overarching story that Artemis is 'She.' This is the pronoun I use when referring to Her too, but I do not believe godds are confined by gender, especially the gender constructs that modern society has created. I bring this up to make my position clear about how I define women: if you say you are a woman, you are. I offer this because I want to widen the audience for Artemis, and I want to reduce the chances of any of my words being taken as being for biological women.

I tried to use language that was more inclusive around the discussion of birth, as not all people who give birth identify as women. I support trans women. I support nonbinary folks. I support those with varied gender histories and ways they want to be seen and known. I recognize language can be harmful and has led to violence against trans and nonbinary folks, especially those of color. However, the sources skew heteronormative. And when quoted, there might be phrases that sound limiting to the broader experience of being a woman or nonbinary being.

I also don't think Artemis would stand for racism, transphobia, sexism, or any oppressive structure.

"She is a person 'at one with herself,' as Esther Harding put it. This is the essence of Artemis, symbolically understood. She is precisely not the feminine counter-part to a masculine divinity; her divinity belongs to herself" (Malamud 57).

Let your divinity belong to you.

(Note: I use 'godds' to honor a more gender-full experience of deities.)

(Additional note: My writing will use She and Her and Herself when referring to Artemis in this book as an act of reverence.)

# Introduction

In the days when I think magick is lacking in the world, all I need to do is close my eyes and think back on my life. All I need to do is to think back to moments that are etched in my brain, simple and straightforward. All I need to do is to take a breath and turn inward.

And there is the trail in the middle of a city in the Midwest. The trail where I would run the same path, again and again, trying to get my body to be able to move without dry heaving. Trying to outrun my anxiety, my fear, and my inability to believe in myself. Like you do. Like I do.

I would run alone, preferring my own company. I wanted to avoid the embarrassment of a body that was learning and to be on my own if I decided that running through the woods wasn't going to happen on a particular day. I wanted to be alone with my fear of the potential for failure.

One day, decades ago, I must have been on the trail early, early enough for dawn to be a desire but not a presence. Following the same red path as I had every other time, I saw a deer. Having grown up in the suburbs, animals were not a thing that I happened upon often. In fact, the most I remember of living creatures was mosquitoes.

The deer was alone, with its head toward the ground, rustling through leaves. It must have been nearly fall, though I don't recall it being cold. This creature turned when it heard me, and I stopped my slow shuffle along the dirt path. Something in my head said I was in the presence of royalty, which didn't make logical sense. Or any sense to me.

My body instinctively settled and I took a long breath to hold the moment in my lungs. I felt myself being called ahead to a new path, though this one was not (entirely) dirt. It was a path of intention, direction, and knowing myself fully.

*Artemis.*

That name rolled off my tongue, as though we were old friends meeting again. But this was the first introduction. Her grounded, steady, knowing energy flowed across my skin and into my wandering heart. I was barely a witch at that time. I was on the cusp of finding out that I was.

And while it's true I may not be remembering this correctly or completely, what I do know is that when I worked with Artemis over 20 years later, it was a homecoming. It was the kind of reconnection that says, "Oh, I'm so glad to see you again. Tell me everything."

# Chapter 1

# Encountering Artemis

### Homeric Hymn to Artemis

*I sing of Artemis, whose shafts are of gold, who cheers on the hounds, the pure maiden, shooter of stags, who delights in archery, own sister to Apollo with the golden sword. Over the shadowy hills and windy peaks she draws her golden bow, rejoicing in the chase, and sends out grievous shafts. The tops of the high mountains tremble and the tangled wood echoes awesomely with the outcry of beasts: earth quakes and the sea also where fishes shoal. But the goddess with a bold heart turns every way destroying the race of wild beasts: and when she is satisfied and has cheered her heart, this huntress who delights in arrows slackens her supple bow and goes to the great house of her dear brother Phoebus Apollo, to the rich land of Delphi, there to order the lovely dance of the Muses and Graces. There she hangs up her curved bow and her arrows, and heads and leads the dances, gracefully arrayed, while all they utter their heavenly voice, singing how neat-ankled Leto bare children supreme among the immortals both in thought and in deed.*

*Hail to you, children of Zeus and rich-haired Leto! And now I will remember you and another song also.* Translated by Hugh G. Evelyn-White. The Homeric Hymns

When you find yourself with a godd, it is best to start with getting to know each other, sitting down for tea, and asking questions about why you are both at the table. It is best to start by dropping into the place between time and facts, into the space between what you think you know and what you will come to know.

Let's begin there.

## The 'Trick' of the Wild Ones

I think this can probably be said of many godds, but those beyond the time of humans might not make sense in a modern context. Artemis, for example, with Her ability to be free in the forest might seem hard to 'catch.' There might be moments in your time with Her when you don't know what is happening and what you are meant to do.

You will have questions and might think you are heading down the wrong path. But this is part of the journey. I want you to remember this as you set off for this adventure: your relationship with Artemis can only be defined by you. There is no right or wrong way to do anything in this work. The only thing I suggest is to learn what you can and see what calls your name. Sit with what you learn and sit a while longer until you understand what it offers you in this lifetime. You are here for a reason, and you don't need to know that reason.

Let it be revealed. "Artemis not only enjoys one of the most widespread cults, but is also one of the most individual and manifestly one of the oldest deities" (Burkert 149). She has been in the minds of humans for many years. Perhaps She is coming to you for the same reason someone else at some other time also experienced. Perhaps you are a new part of the stories that have been learned and lived. Perhaps you are the one who needs the wild in ways you cannot imagine. Yet.

## Know Your Intention

I imagine that if you happened upon Artemis in the woods, She would ask you why you were there. Would you have a reason? What is your intention for meeting Her and traveling this path right now? Do you have a clear sense of what has brought you here to this moment?

You don't have to have a clear answer, as sometimes the godds call to us and we can only answer. The reason doesn't become clear until later.

But you might also be a person who has seen the shape of the hunter, and you know why you are here. If you know, I encourage you to write this intention down before you go further. You can use this as a guidepost as this relationship continues (or not). The clearer your intention, the more you may get from this work.

There are hundreds of reasons to seek out the godds. What are yours?

Do you have questions?
Do you have requests?
Do you want to build a relationship?
Do you want to work with them for a short time?
Do you want to work with a deity for a lifetime?

Knowing what you want will help you begin a relationship with clarity and purpose. Of course, things can change (and they often do), but starting with a direction helps to inform what you need to know and what you may need to do next.

## Trust What Happens

Artemis has taught me many things, but the most important lesson is this: trust yourself. While you will make mistakes, you still need to trust yourself as you make decisions in your life. The world often asks us to get confirmation from everyone else on a decision before we reach into our hearts to ask what we want and to believe what we hear.

Instead, take this opportunity and this time to sink into the possibility that you are someone who can trust what you know and what you do. When you trust yourself, you build a relationship that can face all that the wild has to teach you.

There is no time in the hunt to go back and forth about every decision. Claim yourself as the wise one you need when it is time to aim.

If this sounds like too large of a request, that is understandable. Instead, I offer this: do one thing each day for yourself so you can build trust. Make a small daily promise to yourself that you will honor and keep. This might be as simple as brushing your teeth. This might be as complex as a devotional prayer to Artemis. It doesn't matter what it is, so long as you do it. The smallest steps will bring you back to your wild heart. The heart that knows, even when it falters. The heart that shows up again and again.

From this point forward, offer yourself trust. Offer yourself a confident breath. Give yourself the promise that your wild heart can be honored. And it should be. You are worthy of honor.

## Magickal Practice: Trance into the Forest

If you are familiar with trances or meditations, you can settle into a practice that feels right for you. If you are new to this work, I encourage you to read the next section aloud to yourself before you follow the practice. Some find it helpful to read the text aloud while recording it on a device so you can listen and settle in without having to flip through pages.

Find a place where you can feel comfortable and supported. This might be on the ground, in a chair, or moving your body if that is your process. Find a way to make your body feel relaxed. Support the parts of you that need extra support today. Maybe dim the lights or draw the shades. Do this work in a space where you will not be interrupted to sink right into the space of knowing beyond knowing.

If it helps to close your eyes, please do that. If you'd rather soften your gaze, that works too. The goal is to allow yourself to go inward, into yourself to follow the way of your knowing.

Here, you can start to find your breath and how it moves in your lungs. There is no need to change or fix it. There is no need for long breaths unless those feel good to you. Just come into a rhythm that feels right.

Here, I invite you to scan your body for any tension that might be present. You can start at your feet and move up. You can start at your head and move down. Again, whatever works best for you. You might focus on certain areas of your body, feeling into current tension, and then breathe out to release the tension. Or some like to purposefully tense the muscle and then release it to have a deeper effect.

Take your time in this place to fully come into your body and away from the outside world. You may find parts of you remain a little tense, and you can also know they will release when they are ready, as they can.

Once you feel your entire body relax, open your inner eye. You might call this your witch's eye or your inner knowing. Begin to widen and unfurl into a new space. This might be a space that is clear to see, or it might be a feeling in your body. It might be a place of a wide-open field or it might be a relaxing into awareness.

When you feel that you are more open than before, you may begin to sense that you are on a path. And this path takes you from where you are to where you will go. You begin to travel this path because it is familiar, somehow. It feels safe, even if it is dark, even if it is a place you've never been before.

You might begin to sense or hear the rustling of leaves and branches. You might experience the crunch of decay underneath your feet and sense how the trees rise around you. Allow yourself to know the forest as it arrives for you. As it surrounds you in its wonder and grace.

As you move through this space, you may begin to feel as though you're being watched. This is not an unsettling feeling, in fact, it might be a feeling you have been hoping to feel. It might be the experience you have called for. The rustling slows and you turn to find a strong figure in the space before you. You notice the shape of a body, of a being. And you realize who this is. You realize that the one who watches and hunts is Artemis. And She has been hunting you. She has been waiting to see if you would notice Her. And She stops.

At this moment, you can decide to talk with Her and to follow Her. You can decide to listen or witness Her presence. You might decide She is a being who requires gifts or devotional actions. You can follow your heart to understand what She might offer you today.

Take a few minutes to just be with Her. Take a few minutes to have the experience you want and the experience you might need. It may not be something that makes sense. It may not offer you any answers. It might be quick and quiet. All of this is possible.

Enjoy a few moments with Artemis as She arrives right now.

(Wait a few minutes.)

When you feel ready to be done with the experience, it will be time to go. You might use this time to say thanks, offer Her a gift, or ask one more question. But you will need to prepare to go, as you cannot stay in the land of trance forever. Though you can always return.

Begin to make your way back down the path to the place where you began your journey. Maybe the path looks different than it did before. Maybe it looks brighter or darker, or you notice things you may not have sensed on the way. Take it all in, knowing that anything you have experienced will return with you as it needs to.

Once you feel you are back to where you began, you might feel the different parts of your body that you relaxed earlier.

Maybe you begin to move your head a bit from side to side. Maybe you move your shoulders slowly and begin to stretch your back. Maybe you begin to circle your hips and your arms to bring awareness to them. Maybe you begin to shake your hips and legs to bring them back into the present moment. And you might circle your feet around the foot by turning your ankles.

As you return, open your eyes if they have been closed or widen them if they have been half-closed. Look around the room and say your name a few times to bring yourself back. This might be a good time to write anything you want to remember. You might also just sit in the energy and see how it feels in your body.

The first encounter with Artemis can be a moment of recognizing how far you may have strayed from your wildness. And I define wildness as that which is inherently you, outside of the constructs and confines of the overculture. Wildness is the deepest trust in yourself and the deepest knowing. Let Her call you back to it. Join the hunt for yourself again.

# Chapter 2

# The Birth & Family of Artemis

Artemis (Ἄρτεμις) or Diana (Roman name) or Cynthia (from Her birthplace on Mount Cynthus in Delos) was one of many maiden goddesses in Olympus (others were Athena, Aphrodite, and Vesta). She was born of Zeus and Leto. And if you know anything of the Greek godds and the 'adventures' of Zeus, you can probably already guess that She is a goddess that came into this world in a surprising way.

First, I want to note that Artemis' name is not Greek. What seems to be true is that it arrived first on Linear B tablets (late Minoan scripts) in Pylos. It was in this location that it's thought Artemis became linked through "the Mycenaeans with the old goddess of Crete, were legends of the goddesses Diktynna, 'She of the Net,' Britomartis, the 'Sweet Virgin,' and Eileithyia, goddess of childbirth are transferred to Her" (Baring & Cashford 323).

According to the work of Baring and Cashford, at Ephesus in Asia Minor, there was a temple that contained a statue called Artemis. But it was not the Artemis that we often see in art and other images. This Artemis was a large, blackened figure with heads of animals and multiple egg-like breasts. At first glance, this looks more like a fertility goddess, which is not the first thing I think of when considering Artemis. The thought is that She was renamed by the Greeks, and this statue was a different local deity (329).

Like many deities and many goddesses, Artemis might have many names and many places from which She has emerged. And while we might not be able to narrow Her down to one source, is that a surprise with the goddess of the hunt?

## The Birth of Artemis (and Apollo)

Zeus is a godd of many sexual encounters (some consensual and many not) even as he was wed to Hera. Unsurprisingly, Hera was upset when She found out that Zeus had laid with Leto, a Titaness, who was pregnant by him. Hera made it Her mission to travel the world to seek out Leto and punish Her.

Leto traveled as far as She could to seek out a safe place to not only give birth to Artemis but also to give birth to Artemis' twin brother, Apollo. Hera sent a serpent to follow Leto across the world and said that Artemis would not be born in any place in the world where the sun shone. But with the help of the wind, Leto found herself in Delos, where she gave birth to Artemis. And as soon as Artemis was born, She needed to help Her mother give birth to Apollo on the ninth day of her labor.

Artemis was born into a family with great power and history. She was not only the daughter of Zeus, but also the granddaughter of Chronos, Rhea, Coeus, and Phoebe, but She was also a half-sister to Athena, Ares, Hermes, Dionysus, and Persephone.

## Who Is Artemis?

Artemis is an Olympian, a being who has been born from mighty and powerful godds, one who was thrust into the world with purpose and with a voice. She spoke with Zeus when She was just a child to request what She needed. From Her bow and arrows to Her maidenhood and 80 nymphs, She did not hesitate to ask for what She wanted.

*Of Artemis we hymn—no light thing is it for singers to forget her—whose study is the bow and the shooting of hares and the spacious dance and sport upon the mountains; beginning with the time when sitting on her father's knees—still a little maid—she spake these words to her sire [Zeus]: 'Give me to keep my maidenhood, Father, forever: and give me to be of many names, that Phoibos [Apollo] may not vie with me. And give me arrows and a bow–stay, Father, I ask thee not for quiver or for mighty bow: for me the Kyklopes will straightway fashion arrows and fashion for me a well-bent bow. But give me to be Phaesphoria (Bringer of Light) and give me to gird me in a tunic with embroidered border reaching to the knee, that I may slay wild beasts. And give me sixty daughters of Okeanos for my choir–all nine years old, all maidens yet ungirdled; and give me for handmaidens twenty Nymphai Amnisides [of the Amnisos River in Krete] who shall tend well my buskins, and, when I shoot no more at lynx or stag, shall tend my swift hounds. And give to me all mountains; and for city, assign me any, even whatsoever thou wilt: for seldom is it that Artemis goes down to the town. On the mountains will I dwell and the cities of men I will visit only when women vexed by the sharp pang of childbirth call me to their aid–even in the hour when I was born the Moirai ordained that I should be their helper, forasmuch as my mother suffered no pain either when she gave me birth or when she carried me win her womb, but without travail put me from her body.'*

*So spake the child and would have touched her father's beard, but many a hand did she reach forth in vain, that she might touch it [in supplication]. And her father smiled and bowed assent. And as he caressed her, he said: 'When goddesses bear me children like this, little need I heed the wrath of jealous Hera. Take, child, all that thou askest, heartily. Yea, and other things therewith yet greater will thy father give thee. Three times ten cities and towers more than one will I vouchsafe thee–three times ten cities that shall not know to glorify any other god but to glorify the only and be called of Artemis And thou shalt be Watcher over Streets and harbours.'* *So he spake and bent his head to confirm his words.* Translated by Mair. Callimachus, Hymn 3 to Artemis 1 ff

This image of tall, strong Artemis in Her short tunic, with a silver bow and arrows that always aimed true, is the one that shows up most often in stories and myths. She also arrives as a light-bearer with torches in Her hands and the moon and stars around Her head. (Shinoda Bolen 46).

Artemis is committed to the hunt, to be sure, but also the one who can travel between worlds of nature and man to protect the wild, women and children, and the movement of life. But She is also fierce and seems to be rigid in the ways She thinks about the world. There are many stories in which She is seen as committed to chasteness, and so committed that She judges those who choose to lose their virginity.

## The Question of Being a Virgin Goddess

Outside of being seen in art with Her arrows, the idea that Artemis is a virgin goddess is an often-cited attribute of this godd. She is frequently portrayed as being young and maiden-like, in a way that might hint at virginity. While Athena is also known as a virgin, Athena is seen as being an adult, which offers the question: why is Artemis known as the virgin?

According to the Homeric Hymn, it is said that the lovely Aphrodite can stir up the passion of so many godds, but for a few: Athena, Hestia, and Artemis. It is said that Aphrodite cannot

> ...*ever tame in love Artemis the huntress with shafts of gold; for she loves archery and the slaying of wild beasts in the mountains, the lyre also and dancing and thrilling cries and shady woods and the cities of upright men.* Translated by Evelyn-White. Homeric Hymn 5 to Aphrodite 6 ff

And Sappho, a Greek poet, once wrote that even Eros would never approach Artemis. But as Artemis is often considered to be the godd of feminism, Guiley notes:

[Artemis] personifies the positive attributes of the moon, which is the source of Witches' magical power, as well as independence, self-esteem, and fierce aggressiveness. A virgin goddess and maiden warrior, she is the eternal feminist, owned by no man, beholden to none (102).

Indeed, many of Artemis' nymphs were also considered virgins in stories, but when you investigate writings about those who worshipped Artemis, you find something different. You find that this virginity was a sacred promise that was temporary – and not something that was meant to be a lifelong vow.

"At the sanctuary of Artemis at Ephesos, virgin priestesses were allowed to move on to a life of marriage and children following their service" (Breton Connelly 41). This passage further speaks of how virginity was more of a phase than a lifelong condition. The service was meant to be a year-long, and some scholars have noted that virginity was more of a punishment than service or the ideal.

In myth, at least, if a priestess of Artemis lost her virginity, the goddess became angry: when Comaetho, a priestess, and Melanippus used Artemis' sanctuary 'as a bridal chamber,' Artemis' wrath destroyed the people; the earth bore no crops, and there were unusual diseases and inexplicable deaths (Lefkowitz 180 – 181).

In translations, it is often repeated that Artemis asked for Her virginity, though She will also be the one who seems to empower followers to tap into their wildness and sexuality. But in other texts, it is said that Artemis despises sexual intercourse.

As we see her in Western art, Artemis is the virginal moon goddess roaming the forest with her band of nymphs, bearing the bow and quiver, avoiding men and killing any male who looks on her. But this familiar form was only one of the identities assumed by this complex Greek goddess, for she was also the many-breasted Artemis of Ephesus, a semi-human symbol of fecundity, and the warlike Artemis said to have been the special goddess of the Amazons. It is problematic whether she was originally an all-encompassing goddess later divided into separate identities, or if Artemis became so complex by assuming the attributes of lesser goddesses as her worshippers took control of Greece. But, like Isis or Ishtar, Artemis came to represent the variable energies of the feminine. She was therefore contradictory; she was the virgin who promoted promiscuity; she was the huntress who protected animals; she was a tree, a bear, the moon. Artemis was the image of a woman moving through her life and assuming different roles at different times; she was a veritable encyclopedia of feminine possibility (Monaghan 54).

Like so many other deities that seem to be generally accepted and categorized for being one thing, Artemis arrives in story and myth with different facets and interpretations. And one would do well to remember that many godds are portrayed and interpreted the way they are due to the person doing the interpreting. With few translations from women, a translation of who Artemis is should perhaps be taken lightly.

Pomeroy notes:

The Artemis of classical Greece probably evolved from the concept of a primitive mother goddess, and both she and her sister Athena were considered virgins because they had never submitted to a monogamous marriage. Rather, as befits mother goddesses, they had enjoyed many consorts. Their failure to marry, however, was misinterpreted as virginity by succeeding generations of men who considered loss of virginity only with conventional marriage (6).

Those who tell the stories often interpret as they see the world, not as the world is.

## Magickal Practice: What Do You Really Want?

People are drawn to Artemis by the way She speaks up for herself and for what She wants, even as a child of the all-powerful Zeus.

To sink into this practice with Artemis, I encourage you to create an altar for Her. This might be a simple space where you have a picture or a statue of Her. It might contain a branch or an image of a bow and arrow. Or you might have another idea about what She might like to celebrate Her.

Once you have this space, I invite you to sit at this altar for a few minutes a day, perhaps during the ideal times for a hunt, e.g., dawn and dusk. You can light a candle to demonstrate you are doing work with Her. You can create sacred space in the way you like, or you can simply close away the world and focus on arriving in a place of devotion.

After the space feels ready, take out a notebook and write down what you want in your life. It doesn't have to be a long list, as you can repeat this every day. Or you could write down one item each day. What do you really want in your life? Once you have a list, read it to Her – aloud or in your heart. Practice asking for what you really want, even if you don't know if you will ever get it and even if you're not sure you're worthy of it.

This practice is about sitting with a godd and being true to who you are. It is about getting comfortable with asking for what you truly want in your life. With Artemis witnessing this practice, you might just find you start asking for what you want in your everyday life a bit more.

You can leave this list on the altar. Leave it there to soak up the magick that comes from being authentic and true to yourself. You might even put the paper or journal out in the moonlight as a special way to bring attention to your desires.

# Chapter 3

# The Many Visions of Artemis

As the goddess of wildlife, particularly of young wildlife, she was associated with many undomesticated animals that symbolized Her qualities. The stag, doe, hare, and quail all shared her elusive nature. The lioness exemplified her regality and prowess as a hunter, and the fierce boar represented her destructive aspect. The bear was an appropriate symbol for her role as protector of the young (pubescent Greek girls consecrated to Artemis and under her protection were called arktoi or 'female bears' during a tomboy phase of their lives). Finally, the wild horse roamed widely with companions, as did Artemis with Her nymphs (Shinoda Bolen 46)

Though you may not have happened upon Artemis in your daily life, when you consider all the ways She can show up, perhaps you just didn't notice Her. The goddess of the wild is one that cannot be limited. The wild is everywhere and She is everywhere. She is in the coming of the dawn and the glory of the wild beasts. She is also the one who supports births and is present at death. She is all things and all ways of living and dying.

She is unto herself and unto the world. She arrives in many moments of a day and a life, silently and surely.

### Nature

Artemis can seem contradictory. She roams in nature, often described as being in the woods or up in the mountains. She asked Zeus for the mountains so that She might travel in them as She pleases on Her own. At the same time, She also asked for the power of being a giver of light, which translates into the one who can bring the dawn to the sky. However, with the light, She also brings the crop-destroying frost. (Over time, Artemis was less associated with the dawn, with Eos being given that role.)

In some stories, She is said to ruin crops because of injustices She feels have been done to Her. She is quick to destroy that which might feed the animals and humans She protects. While on the one hand, this seems like a strange combination of facts, I wonder if this is an embodiment of the harshness of nature.

Nature can offer resources, but it also fails to provide them, even if you have done all you are supposed to do to grow food or keep the land bountiful. Perhaps Artemis claims the land that She wants as Her own and for herself because She thinks humans are not able to do what needs to be done. But She does. She understands that sometimes things need to die for the greater good, even if it's just Her measure of what is good.

Her actions might serve to encourage long-term change in the way that humans relate to nature and how humans honor those who do want to protect the land. Perhaps this harshness does not intend cruelty, but the intention of demonstrating clear boundaries for what should and should not be done for the wild. Since Artemis does continue to hunt and travel in the lands She was given, Her dedication to nature seems clear. After all, hunting requires nature to support what runs in the woods.

I think of land sovereignty when I think of Artemis. "Land sovereignty is the right of working peoples to have effective access to, use of, and control over land and the benefits of its use and occupation, where land is understood as resource, territory, and landscape."[1]

Artemis asks for nature not because She wants to hoard what is present, but to ensure ongoing access. In this way, She offers us inspiration to do the same in the natural spaces we encounter in our lives. How do the working people continue to maintain access, use, and control over the land and the benefits of its use?

Perhaps Artemis' commitment is not as simple as loving nature and protecting it. The relationship with nature is vital to everyone's ongoing health and well-being, but it can also require hard decisions and actions. I think of the prescribed burns that help to prevent forest fires and how they kill but also protect the future.

There is a sense that the virginity of Artemis and the untouched woods are related, as both being sacred and inviolable. Perhaps punishments are appropriate for violations.

## The Hunt & Wild Beasts

Artemis' prowess in hunting is not only shown in the stories told of Her but also in the ways She is described. Sometimes, She travels in a chariot with two stags pulling Her along, while in other descriptions, She takes the shape of a deer. And while She is most often pictured with a bow, Artemis also made nets to hunt for fish (Weigle 80).

This speaks to the complexity of the hunt. At what point does the chase shift from running toward to running away? How do we hold being the hunter and the hunted? What is the conversation we might have around power and how we wield it?

The male who wishes to honor Artemis must understand that he may neither see nor possess her: there is a core in the mysteries of untouched nature and of femininity that must remain virgin. The woman herself, while providing favorable conditions for the development of this part of her nature, should not pollute it with words, nor implicate it in the process of seduction, nor exploit it in the world of relationships. It is essential to the ecology of human and spiritual values that we re-discover the meaning of an intact femininity and that we multiply, at the same time, the natural reserves of prairies, virgin forests, and spring-waters (Paris 115).

Homer's *Iliad* describes, "...Artemis herself had taught him [a hunter] to strike down every wild thing that grows in the mountain forests" (Baring and Cashford 324). Those ancient Greeks who were successful in their hunts would hang the skin and horns on a tree or other space to honor the blessing of Artemis.

Artemis as the goddess of the hunt and the wild heart is a being that requires discernment in the hunt. There is a ritual in the practice of hunting, a sacred relationship between hunter and hunted, and the protection of the goddess for either side. In this way, Artemis can decide who is favored on a day. And even though She might celebrate the hunt, She also protects women during childbirth to ensure they are safe from being hunted.

It is important to note that Artemis is a huntress who is often said to shoot Her arrows from far away, preferring to spend Her time with animals than with humans (Pomeroy 5). Her reverence and preference for animals over humans might help to explain how harsh She can be with humans.

## Moon

In a fragment by Aeschylus, Artemis is described as "the glance of her starry eye" (Baring and Cashford 328). Associated with the moon, She travels in the night for Her hunts, and with Her virginity, Artemis is connected to the New Moon.

The phases of the moon may be connected to how animals move.[2] This would impact the way a hunt would go as animals are more or less active during different periods of the month. While the measured impact of the moon phase seems small, research states that the new moon is best for hunting animals during the day, while the full moon is best for hunting at night.

In addition, there are conversations about the moon and its connection to pregnancy and childbirth.

*Chrysippus in his Old Physics [C3rd B.C.], shows that Artemis is Selene (the Moon) and credits it with an influence on childbirth, says that at the full moon not only do women have the easiest labour but all animals have an easy birth.* Translated by Campbell. Scholiast on Homer's Iliad (Vol. Greek Lyric I Alcaeus Fragment 390)

Though Artemis is associated with the New Moon, it would make sense that the moon cycles (or menstrual cycles) of those who bear children would also be under Her watch to ensure a successful birth.

While there are disagreements about whether Artemis was always connected with the moon, Weigle speaks of a potential connection through the family line. Her mother, Leto, is the child of the Titan Coeus and Phoebe, who may have been a moon goddess herself. A common epithet for Artemis is Phoebe, which speaks to this link and, thus, the connection to the moon (161).

Several scholars point to how Artemis is often connected to and might be the same being as Hecate at one point in history, as found in images, though the two are later separated. It can become confusing as several goddesses are related to the moon: Selene (Full Moon) or Demeter (Full Moon) and Hecate (Dark Moon). However, with the maiden energy of Artemis, Her newness arrives in a crescent, much like the one She is pictured as having on a crown. By the light of the moon, She arrives.

## Protection

The common theme in Artemis' stories is Her ability and willingness to be a protector. She serves to protect those who are being hunted or those who are prepubescent. In ancient Greek times, the godds were seen as being very active in the lives of humans. They were interested and often prone to meddling (see any description of nearly any godd in the Greek pantheon).

The world today often looks to myths to inform and inspire change. When I think of Artemis, I can see how She has been connected to the protection of women and how that might apply to the ongoing debate about reproductive rights.

> Artemis forbids the hunter to wound an animal instead of killing it, leaving it to go its way limping and suffering. In the same way, if one values the integrity of life, one must sacrifice the fetus already marked by the rejection and hostility of those who should receive it with love (Paris 141).

Following this thought, I think Artemis would be a protector of women – all women. She who hunts and is the hunted, is self-possessed and not bound to the opinions or wiles of those who wish to control Her. This includes abortion and birth control to help those who might birth children have a choice in the matter.

It is easy to think that abortion is a choice that is simple and selfish. It is common to hear that argument from those who seek to prevent abortions from being legal and accessible. It is common to hear that women (and those identifying as women and/or those who can give birth) should not be making decisions for their health and their bodies. I would imagine Artemis has something to say about that. While I don't think this is a simple discussion, and there are intersections to consider, I think Artemis would be alongside protestors today, bow and arrow at the ready. I think She fights for the right to make choices.

## Maidens

Along with the energy of virginity is the desire of Artemis to have maidens with Her, so important is this that She asks Zeus when She is a child. She asks for 60 maidens to be part of Her choir, all nine years old and 'ungirdled.' In addition, She requests 20 handmaidens to tend Her boots.

*[I, the maiden daughter of Otreus] was caught up from the dance of huntress Artemis of the golden arrows (khryselakatos) strong-voiced (keladeinos). There were many of us, Nymphai (girls) and marriageable (cattle-earning) maidens, playing together; and an innumerable company encircled us.* Translated by Evelyn-White. Homeric Hymn 5 to Aphrodite 115 ff

The stories of Artemis and Her maidens speak of the singing, of a lyre being played, and the group gathering to dance. This seems to be a celebration of youth and being sovereign. This is a space that is cultivated to allow women to be with one another, to offer support to each other, and to recognize the beauty of the natural world with each other.

In modern times, I look to these maidens as the community we need to cultivate to support us in the 'hunt' of life. I also see this as a reminder that play and joy are just as important to the seriousness of the world in which we live. Plus, there is strength in groups and communities. This group would be more powerful in their shared devotion.

## Sacrifice

"It is not only animal sacrifice that is attributed to Artemis. In the most distant times of Greek religious history, she was associated with the practice of human sacrifice" (Paris 120).

Sacrifice is a loaded word. With its roots in 'sacred' and 'holy,' I often think of sacrifice as a way to make something holy, whether it is myself or a practice. By releasing something, I step into a different relationship, I commit in a way that requires I let go of something else.

One thing I find is not widely discussed about Artemis is the way that hunters would atone for their actions by making blood offerings to Her. In one story of Iphigenia, a virgin who is described as one who sings in her father's (Agamemnon) halls, is going to be a sacrifice to Artemis, as Artemis has demanded it.

Iphigenia begs her brother and her father not to let this happen, and even Achilles steps in to stop this from occurring. But then Iphigenia asks to be the sacrifice, as she believes it will help to save more people and save her homeland. Later, the story of Iphigenia would shift away from what the sacrifice looked like, as human sacrifices were frowned upon, and perhaps storytellers wanted to show Artemis in a more favorable light. In fact, the story would have Iphigenia turn into a deer when she was fatally stabbed. And it was pronounced a miracle.

Scholars have noted that these sacrifices may also have been recounted in stories to show that matriarchal societies would do this without any reasoning outside of being an action required from the goddess. Perhaps they thought these references might serve as a warning of the power of women in groups.

Before the battle of Marathon, the Athenians were anxious about going against the Persian army and promised to sacrifice a she-goat to Artemis for every Persian they killed. However, when it came time to uphold this promise, there were not enough she-goats available. So, the Athenians promised to sacrifice 500 she-goats annually, a practice that continued for 100 more years (Garland 200).

There are other places where Artemis requires blood from hunts or other suitable sacrifices. And if we also look at Artemis and Her followers as leading lives of virginity, that too can be a sacrifice.

## Amazons

Amazons are often envisioned as less civilized than the Greeks. They practice an orgiastic religion, worshiping Ares, the Phrygian Magna Mater, Cybele, and the virginity-loving Artemis in a fashion that recalls the dangerous attraction of Greek women to the worship of Dionysus (Fantham et al 134).

Along with Her maidens or nymphs, Artemis is connected to the Amazons. This seems an obvious connection as the Amazons have been described as women who are untamed and virginal, but also warriors. Often, the stories told of the Amazons seem to be making light of these women. However, the ongoing presence of the Amazons in history and stories seems otherwise. Some describe Artemis as the patron of the Amazons. And some research seems to suggest that a temple at Ephesus was built for Artemis and built by the Amazons.

Even at this moment, you probably already have a picture of them in your head: armored women with spears and bows with arrows. You might picture them on horseback and living on an island without men. But wait, isn't that another story that seems to be reflecting what researchers have found out about the Amazons? Yes. Wonder Woman.

Wonder Woman's name is Diana, the Roman name for Artemis. This heroine not only lives on an island with women, training for battle and having little interest in men, Wonder Woman seems a modern retelling of this strong, sensual woman who will fight for what is right. And she will kill if it is necessary.

Paris asks the question best, "In a patriarchal society, is it inevitable that any group of women who show a forcible desire to separate and establish well-defended boundaries be considered a threat?" (158) While Artemis may not have been a part of the Amazons, I can see how this sisterhood of strong women would turn to this goddess for aid and support.

## Magickal Practice: Tapping into Your Own Wild Heart
You can relate to Artemis by finding yourself in the wild. Travel out into places that are away from people and responsibilities. If you are not in a place to do this, you can also find Her wildness between sidewalk cracks and the insistence of nature among the concrete. Or you can find pictures and videos of the wild online to help you travel outside of where you are.

Once you have arrived in a place of the wild, I invite and encourage you to open up your senses. You might look around. You might close your eyes to hear or smell things. You might choose to touch the plants and ground. You might choose to open your mouth to begin to taste the air.

However you choose, find a place that is comfortable for you. Find a place that you can return to regularly. If possible, daily practice is best, but we are not all able to have such access. When you are doing this work inside, you can find a specific video or picture you return to, as well as a way that you sit and be with this space.

As you find your place and space, sit and take it all in. Take in the way the light falls, the way the temperature changes, and the way that things move when you're sitting there. Become a part of the place and become a part of the wild. Notice how things interact with you – or don't. Notice how you interact with the wild – or don't.

It can help to allow anything you were thinking about before to fall to the ground. Step into the present with a breath, by settling your heart, or by relaxing your chest. Once you arrive in a quieter place, you might sense the way your awareness can expand from your body. There is no need to move, just feel the way your awareness can unfold from where you are and out into the space you are in.

Notice what happens when you widen and expand. Notice how much more you can perceive and know. Notice how close you are to the wild and the unexpectedness of it all. Some people like to document what they notice as they notice it, or you can wait until you are done to write down what stood out to you.

It helps to stay in this wild wideness for a few minutes to sense all that you like, but there is no specific timeframe that is best. I would only suggest you stay long enough to sense into the wild, but also not so long that you lose interest. Once you begin to get distracted, and you will, in the beginning, you can bring your awareness back into your body and slowly return to the present moment.

This is a practice of connecting with the wild, as you are always a part of the wild. The world might tell you otherwise, but you are just as much of the forests as you are in them. When you can practice connecting in, you will begin to find your own wild heart – and all that it knows and can teach you.

# Chapter 4

# Artemis Stories & Myths

*Her faithful and the poets call her the Savage or the Queen of the Wild Beasts.*

*Her pleasure is to travel to the woods and the high crags battered by the winds.*

*She loves those animals which have not been subjugated by man.*

*The games of childhood and the chaste thoughts of adolescents belong to her.*

*She is the Invincible Virgin, fierce and beautiful.*

*She is pure and cold, like the light of the moon that guides the hunter through the forest.*

*Her arrow is cruel, sure, and swift.*

*She is the Goddess of untouched Nature, of intact bodies, of hearts free from passion*

Les Dieux de la Grece, Andre Bonnard

Just as we learn the stories of others to get to know them, I find it helps to hear the stories of the godds to find out more about who they are. While stories are often interpretations of what has happened, they can still allow us to better know how to relate with godds. And how the godds can teach us about ourselves in our own stories. When possible, I encourage devotees to seek out original source material and texts, as well as to note differences between translations done by different translators.

## Artemis & Orion

The story of Artemis and Orion is the first story I learned of Her. I was part of a witch camp in Canada, and the theme of the week was this story.

I know this story as beginning with Artemis in the forest, where She would always hunt and find joy in running from place to place. Once, She found herself running and heard someone else in the forest with Her. She was unsure who this was and what they were doing, after all, She was used to hunting alone.

So, She hunted this person and asked them what they were doing in the forest. It was Orion, another being who loved to hunt. Finding their commonality, they became the best of friends and started to hunt together. But Artemis' brother, Apollo, was not pleased with this new relationship. He began to suspect that Artemis and Orion were more than friends.

Artemis insisted that She and Orion were just friends, but Apollo had made up his mind about Orion. Apollo asked to meet up with Orion and they talked about Artemis. Again, Orion was clear that he was only Artemis' friend and had not defiled the virgin goddess. (And honestly, wouldn't Artemis have protected Herself?) In this version of the story, there is a sense that Apollo and Orion became more than friends after this exchange, that perhaps Apollo used his charms to seduce Orion as a manipulation.

Apollo was so upset with Orion (perhaps because Orion revealed Apollo's queerness?) that he sent a monster to Orion's dreams, a scorpion. To escape the monster, Orion ran out into the ocean, where he was safe.

In the meantime, Apollo told Artemis that one of Her nymphs was being attacked by a monster in the ocean. Furious, Artemis took Her bow, loaded an arrow, and shot the monster, who was actually Orion. Artemis killed someone She loved, and to honor him, She placed him in the stars – now as the constellation.

In other versions, Artemis and Orion were closer than friends. According to D'Este, some stories say Orion gets killed by Gaia's scorpion because Orion boasted he could kill anything on earth. Another version of this story by Ovid talks of the scorpion trying to kill Leto first, but Orion tried to save

Leto and was killed in the process. Then Leto placed Orion in the stars for saving her (D'Este 41).

No matter the translation and the characters, the story of Orion and Artemis is layered with themes of friendship, jealousy, and mistakes. The way I hold this story is to think about each character and how they impacted the outcome. Whether Apollo was a jerk or Orion was boastful, they all had parts to play in what happened. Even Artemis was not without fault in these stories. After all, if She had stopped to find out if the story of Her nymph was true, She could have saved Her dear Orion. But instead, She seems to have shot in anger or retaliation, which is a lesson for someone whose aim always makes its target.

## Artemis & Persephone

*[Persephone relates the tale of her abduction to Demeter:] 'All we were playing in a lovely meadow, Leukippe and Phaino and Elektra and Ianthe [and various other Okeanides]...with Pallas [Athena] who rouses battles and Artemis delighting-in-arrows (iokheaira): we were playing and gathering sweet flowers in our hands, soft crocuses mingled with irises and hyacinths, and rose-blooms and lilies, marvellous to see [when she was lured away from their company with a narcissus flower and seized by Haides].'* Translated by Evelyn-White. Homeric Hymn 2 to Demeter 415 ff

According to several translations, in the story of Persephone (Kore) where she is abducted by Hades to go to the underworld, not only is Persephone picking flowers but she is also joined by Athena and Artemis. This makes sense as they are the ones portrayed as virginal maidens. In other stories, Aphrodite is with these maidens when Hades comes and takes Persephone.

Later in the Eleusinian Mysteries, Demeter searches for Persephone with the help of Artemis, but the Eleusians called

Her Hecate. But today, most agree that Hecate is a separate goddess versus a version of Artemis. In addition, sometimes this story includes Iris as being the one who travels with Demeter, so these variations might depend on the translation and the context of the translation.

## Artemis & Hippolytus

*[Hippolytos, a devotee of Artemis, is slain by his father Theseus by the will of Aphrodite:] Diana [Artemis] howled indignation. 'There's no cause to grieve.' Coronides [Asklepios son of Koronis] says. 'I'll restore the pious youth to life, unwounded, and the grisly fates will yield to my art.' At once he takes some herbs from an ivory box. They worked before on the ghost of Glaucus, when an augur resorted to herbs he'd noticed, and a serpent used the help of a serpent. He daubed his breast three times, thrice spoke healing words. The youth raised his drooping head from the ground. The grove and recesses of Dictynna's [Artemis'] wood hide him: he is Virbius of Aricia's lake. Clymenus [Haides] and Clotho resent the threads of life respun and death's royal rights diminished. Jove [Zeus] feared the precedent and aimed his thunderbolt at the man who employed excessive art.* Translated by Boyle. Ovid, Fasti 6. 735 ff

Beyond the hunt of Artemis was Her devotion to those who honored Her. When Hippolytus wanted to be devoted to a chaste life and Artemis, he refused to worship Aphrodite. The goddess of love then made his stepmother fall in love with him. But in doing so, some events led to Hippolytus' death after a fall from a chariot. Artemis saw Hippolytus' devotion and called on Asclepius, the god of Medicine, to help resurrect Hippolytus to become Virbius, a man who ruled in Italy. We see here that Artemis likes to honor and help those who dedicate themselves to Her and how She thinks life should be lived.

## Artemis & Hera

*[In the conflict of the gods over Troy, Apollon declined to join battle with Poseidon:] But his sister, Artemis of the wild (agrotera), lady of wild beasts (potnia theron), scolded him bitterly and spoke a word of revilement: 'You run from him, striker from afar. You have yielded Poseidon the victory entire. He can brag, where nothing has happened. Fool, then why do you wear that bow, which is wind and nothing. Let me not hear you in the halls of my father boasting ever again, as you did before among the immortals, that you could match your strength in combat against Poseidon.'*

*So she spoke, but Apollon who strikes from afar said nothing to her; but [Hera] the august consort of Zeus, full of anger, scolded the lady of the showering arrows in words of revilement: 'How have you had the daring, you shameless hussy, to stand up and face me? It will be hard for you to match your strength with mine even if you wear a bow, since Zeus has made you a lion among women, and given you leave to kill any at your pleasure. Better for you to hunt down the ravening beasts in the mountains and deer of the wilds, than try to fight in strength with your betters. But if you would learn what fighting is, come on. You will find out how much stronger I am when you try to match strength against me.'*

*She spoke, and caught both of her arms at the wrists in her left hand then with her own bow, smiling, boxed her ears as Artemis tried to twist away, and the flying arrows were scattered. She got under and free and fled in tears, as a pigeon in flight from a hawk wings her way into some rock-hollow and a cave, since it was not destiny for the hawk to catch her. So she left her archery on the ground, and fled weeping...Leto picked up the curved bow and the arrows which had fallen in the turn of the dust one way and another. When she had taken up the bow she went back to her daughter. But the maiden came to the bronze-founded house on*

*Olympos and the ambrosial veil trembled about her. Her father Kronides [Zeus] caught her against him, and laughed softly, and questioned her: 'Who now of the Ouraniones (Heavenly Ones), dear child, has done such things to you, rashly, as if you were caught doing something wicked?'*

*Artemis sweet-garlanded lady of clamours (eustephanos keladeine) answered him: 'It was your wife, Hera of the white arms, who hit me, father, since hatred and fighting have fastened upon the immortals.'* Homer, Iliad 21. 470 ff

Even the mighty huntress, Artemis, is hurt by Hera during the Trojan War. After getting upset with Her brother for not taking sides, Artemis is blamed for the arrows that Apollo sends off in the battle. Because Artemis is committed to being an ally of the Trojans, this does not please everyone. Hera is so upset with Artemis for this and the shower of arrows that she fires hits Her ears, causing Artemis to run away in tears to Zeus. Once more, it appears that miscommunication between Apollo and Artemis has caused trouble for Artemis.

## When You See Artemis

In the stories of Artemis, Her virginity was celebrated while also being something that needed to be protected at all costs. Many stories show Artemis taking revenge on those who might have seen Her unclothed. For example, when Actaeon saw Artemis, She turned him into a stag and had his hounds chase him and rip him apart. Or when Siproites saw naked Artemis, She turned him into a girl.

These stories (and others) tell me that Artemis is someone who wants to be in control of herself at all times. One might say She is very committed to consensual interactions and is a fierce protector of bodily autonomy.

## The Fate of Callisto / Kallisto

Even Kallisto/Callisto, one of Artemis' hunting companions, was punished for not acting in a way that Artemis deemed appropriate.

*Hesiod says she [Kallisto] was the daughter of Lycaon and lived in Arcadia. She chose to occupy herself with wild-beasts in the mountains together with Artemis, and, when she was seduced by Zeus, continued some time undetected by the goddess, but afterwards, when she was already with child, was seen by her bathing and so discovered. Upon this, the goddess was enraged and changed her into a beast. Thus she became a bear and gave birth to a son called Arkas...but [later] Zeus delivered her because of her connection with him and put her among the stars, giving her the name Bear (Arktos) because of the misfortune which had befallen her.* Translated by Evelyn-While. Hesiod, The Astronomy Fragment 3

It makes sense that Artemis has clear boundaries about what is right (for Her) and what is wrong (for others). As with any deity, I think it wise to maintain curiosity about more complicated stories to see what they might offer to broaden understanding when building a relationship.

## Magical Practice: What Is the Story You Carry?

Just as Artemis carries a bow and a quiver of arrows, so do we carry stories that can save or harm. We have the power to save ourselves and to hurt ourselves each day. Instead of being the one who acts before thinking, let's consider a practice of discernment.

What you will need:

Timer
Paper
Pen or pencil

Before you begin, think about a story you tell about your life. It can help to think about a time when you were a hero or a victim, as this can help you see a story more clearly. While it's not always as simple as that, I encourage you to come back to this practice with more stories once you have tried it for the first time. The best story to work with is the one that you seem to tell in your head over and over. It might be the story that you tell about yourself or someone else.

Once you have this in your head, set the timer for 5 minutes. Take the paper and pen and start writing the story down from your perspective.

- What did you see?
- What did you experience?
- What did it feel like?
- How does the story impact you today?

Set a time to see how long it takes to write down everything you can. This might take 5 minutes, or it might take 20. The point is to write without thinking too hard and just get it all on paper.

Once you're done, stretch your hands and wrists. Move your body a bit to loosen up any tightness that might have happened because of retelling this story.

Then set the timer for the same amount of time you needed for the first story to be told. Now write down the story from another perspective. Maybe it's the person that caused harm or maybe it's from the perspective of someone else in your life looking from the outside. Think about what it might have looked like for then.

- What might they have felt when seeing this story?
- What might they have thought about you when hearing about this story?

- Or, if they were a part of the story, how did this story impact their lives?

When you're done, take a few moments to rest and integrate what you've experienced.

- What does it feel like to consider different angles?
- What does it mean to look at things from another perspective?
- Did the story feel different after you thought about it in a new way?
- Did your feelings change?
- How do you feel about the other people in the story?

What you may find is that you can widen into compassion when you think about different perspectives. And when you can do this, you might aim accurately the next time you need to shoot your bow.

# Chapter 5

# Artemis & Health

*[Artemis] send gentle peace, and health with lovely hair, and to the*
*mountains drive disease and care.* Translated by Taylor. Orphic
Hymn 36 to Artemis

The name, Artemis, comes from the word artemês, meaning
healthy, vigorous, and uninjured. She is the one who can offer
good health and strength to others. Artemis herself is strong
enough to fight and hunt and is associated with the cycle of life:
birth, illness, and sudden death.

There are stories of how Artemis cares for those who support
Her, helping to heal them from injury and illness. Frequently,
Artemis is shown as someone who will give favors to those who
worship Her.

*But on whomsoever thou [Artemis] lookest smiling and gracious...*
*neither do they go to the tomb, save when they carry thither the aged.*
Translated by Mair. Callimachus, Hymn 3 to Artemis 128 ff

It is said that She makes people safe and sound, or *Artemeas*, a
term coined by Strabo, a Greek historian/writer.[3] May She also
offer you places of safety and ease.

## Birth

The function of Artemis is to preserve the purity of life. She
guards life so that it will not be diminished, wounded or
degraded. But she who has the power to aid the women in
childbirth has also the power, by her whistling arrow, to
bring sudden death (Paris 139).

Artemis is first associated with birth as She helped to birth Her own brother when Leto was in labor for nine days and fleeing the wrath of Hera. However, outside of this story, Artemis' connection to helping women in childbirth is not emphasized in myths.

In the daily life of ancient Greece, children were born at home or in nature. There were no obstetricians or labor and delivery teams. Doctors were only called upon if the woman was in trouble and needed extra help. And even then, since most doctors were men, it was thought to be shameful to call on them, as the woman should be able to birth without help beyond midwives.

Artemis was present at births, though there are thoughts She would be angry at the idea of sexual intercourse (not all translations and interpretations, but some). "It was necessary to appease the goddess' anger by invoking Her in prayer before delivery and by dedicating clothing in Her shrine afterward" (Garland 89).

As a side note, there seems to be enough information to show that abortions were performed in these times, but that certain cases of abortions were frowned upon and would lead to the household being polluted by death (Garland 91). There were also situations in which abortion was seen as a criminal act.

While this begins to sound as though Artemis is not the person to be by your side at childbirth, it is also wise to note that She began as a sort of midwife to Her brother and was perfect for this role because of Her instinctual nature.

*'Once I felt this thrill of pain in my womb. I cried out for Artemis in heaven, who loves the hunt and whose care relieves those giving birth. She came to me then and eased me'* (Euripides 165-8).

I offer that birth and bringing life into the world are conscious actions, to a point. It is a rite of passage that requires surrender.

Birthing a human might be simpler with the medicalization of delivery today, but at its core, birth is the act of giving over to whatever is happening. You need to be present for what is needed and, from what I hear, there is a point where you don't think you can go on. But you do because you must. Because you need to. A metaphor for life altogether and a metaphor for anything that requires you to sacrifice a part of yourself. Of course, Artemis is there.

## Death & Disease

Unlike more traditional godds of death and the underworld, Artemis kills. I wonder why this is not spoken of more often regarding Her. Perhaps it is not unlike how people talk about Aphrodite as being 'only' the goddess of love and beauty. But even Aphrodite is rageful, jealous, and vindictive. Artemis can also be complex and contradictory.

There are parts of *The Odyssey* that speak of Artemis killing people with Her arrows. In *The Iliad*, Artemis is described as given the right by Her father, Zeus, to kill anyone at 'Her pleasure.' Artemis responds to those who do not seem to respect Her. In one story, She killed Chione or aimed an arrow at Her tongue, rendering Chione mute.

As another example of Artemis' vengefulness, we hear of Adonis boasting about his ability to hunt better than Artemis (or possibly as revenge for the death of Hippolytus), which led to his death by a wild boar She sent to him.

Still another story brings Artemis and Apollo together to kill Niobe's (queen of Thebes) children. Apparently, Niobe criticized Leto, Artemis and Apollo's mother, which did not make the twins very happy. They killed each of the children with poisoned arrows. (Though some stories say some survived.) Unsurprisingly, Niobe was upset and wept for Her losses. It is said that in seeing this, Artemis turned Her to stone.

Even with these stories, there were some, like Penelope, who asked for a swift death from Artemis. And it is also said that in some places where there is no disease, Artemis or Apollo visit the people to bring their death. One might say that sudden and unexpected deaths might be the blessing (or curse) of Artemis. Artemis is connected with illness and disease, which might begin or hasten the dying process.

In some conversations about Artemis, She is linked with causing the sudden death of infants, girls, and women. And the paradox continues. She who protects also destroys.

## Healing

After learning of the way Artemis hastens death, it might seem hard to transition to the way She is also associated with health. Like any being, there are many parts of this godd and Her impact in the stories shared of Her.

Even in healing, Artemis seems to step in when the one dying or injured acts favorably toward Her. She is especially helpful with those who have been bitten by a rabies-infected dog. Her honor for the wild extends into compassion for a human hurt by animals. I imagine Artemis sees the human as an unfortunate victim of a diseased animal and takes pity on both the animal and the human.

Artemis and Her brother Apollo are described as deities of health and healing. Those who were devoted to Artemis would often bring their animals to Her to prevent disease and to make sure they were healthy for slaughter.

Within *The Illiad*, Artemis is described as helping Leto with healing Aineias after being hurt in battle. Artemis is also described in the Orphic Hymn 36:

*[Artemis] send gentle peace, and health with lovely hair, and to the mountains drive disease and care.* Translated by Taylor. Orphic Hymn 36 to Artemis

The contradiction seems to be: Artemis can heal but doesn't always choose to do so. She and Her brother might be blessed with this gift, but they will only use it in certain circumstances. And there are far more stories of them causing death and spreading disease.

Though this is not something that is proven, I wonder if the emphasis on killing and death is influenced by the translations of the text. After all, to make a strong woman someone who is just focused on death and retaliation makes Her someone who is to be feared instead of celebrated for Her power and ability. But maybe that's just me. It's only recently that the translation of *The Odyssey* and (soon, I heard at the time of writing) *The Illiad* will be completed by women. The stories may shift with new eyes and closer looks.

## Magickal Practice: Calling on Artemis for Guidance

*Note: This is not a practice to replace any advice or treatment recommended by your physician or healthcare professional. I am not a healthcare professional. If you experience and have been diagnosed with any health-related issues, please seek out medical advice first.*

With the powers that Artemis offers and the dedication you show to Her by being open to a relationship, I want to offer a healing practice. This might be a practice you return to after you are deeper in your relationship with Her, or you might come to this early to see if She is open to this sort of work with you.

While this book is about Artemis, Her brother, Apollo, was also well-versed in healing, so you might choose to call upon him during this practice if desired.

Health is something that looks different for everyone. It is not something that can be easily quantified or even measured. After all, tests might say you are out of balance, and you might feel well. Or you might have a body that will always cause tests to look different from 'normal.' You get to decide what health means to you in this practice.

What is fair to say, I think, is that health is an ongoing and personal conversation. It is finding the activities and energies that support your lifeforce. If you feel out of balance, this can be restorative to your body, mind, and soul.

It is best to cleanse your body before ritual. You don't have to take any special baths, though you might choose to do so. Sometimes, I just wash my face, hands, and feet to prepare for magick. I would also encourage you to set up a more extensive altar with offerings to Artemis. This will help you show your devotion, and it will show how you honor Her. You might bring food as part of the modern hunt or things that honor Her power and strength. I have a naturally shed deer antler on my altar to Her during working like this. And I will often dress as someone ready for a hunt to align with the energy.

Of course, every relationship is different, so you can choose what works best for you and Her. What is important is that you have something you can promise to Her in return for Her help. This might be that you will light a candle at Her altar each day, or you will honor animals. Find something valuable that requires energy and time of you. And make sure you can follow through!

Once you have prepared a space and once you have allowed yourself to sink into the energy of this ritual, I encourage you to close your eyes and travel the space of your body. Notice what might need healing. Notice what often requires supportive care. Notice where there might be pain or discomfort. If you are not feeling anything now, you can travel to your body to places where pain has lived and lingered.

After you have identified the place of focus, I encourage you to call out to Artemis.

Artemis, oh wondrous one
You of wildness and power

You of knowing and action
You who follows the cycle of life from birth to death
You who harms and heals
I call to you to offer me your advice
I call to you to offer me your guidance
I ask of you and I beseech you to aid me with my healing
I promise to honor you and to make offerings to you
I promise to [insert the promise you will make to Her]
I listen and wait for your wisdom

Once you feel She is present, sit in silence. This is not a moment for you to ask what you want. Let this be a moment where you might hear what you need to hear: instructions, warnings, directives, etc. Allow the moment to inform you and stay here until you feel things are complete.

When you are done, make sure to thank Artemis for what you have received and reiterate your promise to Her. You might offer Her something else, like a piece of your hair or a cup of water. Whatever seems appropriate at the moment and aligned with the gifts you were given.

Allow the sacred space to be released and settled.

*Note: When offered wisdom from a godd, know that you don't always have to do everything they ask or suggest. You are still a human with boundaries and abilities. A beloved mentor of mine always said, "Body trumps spirit." You are still in choice. But when you do take on the wisdom of a godd, be clear in upholding your promises to them. And even if their wisdom suggested something you cannot do now, keep up your promises for at least a moon cycle to show respect.*

# Chapter 6

# Symbols & Offerings

Artemis is the Goddess of untamed nature. Among the rustic people, she is the most popular Goddess in Greece. 'Where has Artemis not danced?' is a Greek saying. Central to her worship are ecstatic dances and the sacred bough, most probably derived from worship of the ancient moon tree, source of immortality, secret knowledge, and wisdom (Spretnak 75).

When looking for ways to bring the energy of Artemis into your life, it can help to ground your focus in the symbols and offerings most associated with Her. Although as you get to know Her and you get to work with Her, you might find you use different items to better serve your relationship.

## Bow & Arrows

In most depictions of Artemis, you will find Her with a bow and a quiver of arrows. In some sources, there are gold and silver arrows, each with its own meaning. She can be seen with a gold bow and arrows, which She has always had. But it is also said that Cyclops gave Artemis silver arrows, seemingly to help Her protect others. Gold arrows were used not only to slay beasts in the mountains but also to bring disease, plague, and sudden death to women. Some translations speak of Apollo as being the one who had the golden bow and Artemis as having the silver bow, as She is associated with the moon.

Artemis asked for these tools and weapons from Zeus. The arrows can be seen as both. While they can harm others, they can also be the right tool to protect and save others.

When working with Artemis, it is helpful to recognize that how you use a tool is just as important as what it is and what it could be used for. But, also, to maintain awareness of how tools can become weapons.

## Dress & Accessories

Artemis is pictured as tall, with a knee-length dress or a full-length robe called a chiton. Sometimes She would have a cloak, as well as some sort of headdress or headband. In art, Artemis will have a crown with a crescent to showcase Her connection to the moon. In other Greek art images, She might have deer pelts on Her shoulders. And She drives a chariot pulled by four golden-horned deer or wild beasts, in some descriptions. She travels with a pack of seven hunting dogs. Artemis dresses in hunting gear of various combinations. Sometimes, She has a spear in addition to or instead of Her bow and arrows.

Some depictions of Artemis also show Her holding a torch or torches, much like Hecate. This might be due to the time period when they seemed to overlap before they separated into two distinct figures. In one of the temples to Artemis, there are two images of Her, one with arrows and one with torches.

When you see images of Artemis, you might also come upon Her carrying a lyre, which alludes to Her singing and dancing with nymphs, but there are few literary references to this instrument.

## Animals

Artemis is most often associated with deer, as part of the hunt. Most important to Artemis was an immortal, golden-horned deer, Cerynitian Hind. This deer was one of the 12 labors of Hercules.

*His [Herakles] third labour was to bring back alive to Mykenai the Elaphos Kerynitis (Cerynitian Hind). It was at Oinoe, a golden-horned deer sacred to Artemis. In his desire neither to kill nor to wound it, Herakles spent a whole year pursuing it. Finally the animal tired of the chase and took refuge on the mountain known as Artemision, and from there proceeded to cross the Ladon River. As it was crossing, Herakles got it with an arrow, hoisted it on his shoulders pressed on urgently through Arkadia. Artemis along with Apollon accosted him on the way, reached for the Hind, and berated him for trying to kill her sacred animal. But Herakles pleaded necessity and said that Eurystheus was to blame, and thus soothed the goddess' wrath; and he brought the animal still living to Mykenai.* Pseudo-Apollodorus, Bibliotheca 2. 81 (trans. Aldrich) (Greek mythographer C2nd A.D.)

The bear also arrives in stories about Artemis, as a sacred companion, in a story that leads to unfortunate consequences for Athenians.

*Women playing the bear used to celebrate a festival for Artemis [at Brauron] . . . The reason was that a wild She-bear [sacred to Artemis] used to come to the deme of Phlauidoi and spend time there; and she became tamed and was brought up with the humans. Some virgin was playing with her and, when the girl began acting recklessly, the She-bear was provoked and scratched the virgin; her brothers were angered by this and speared the She-bear, and because of this a pestilential sickness fell upon the Athenians. When the Athenians consulted the oracle [the god] said that there would be a release from the evils if, as blood price for the She-bear that died, they compelled their virgins to play the bear.* Translated by Suda On Line. Suidas s.v. Arktos e Brauroniois

Other animals of importance include:

- Boar / Wild Boar
- Fish (freshwater)

- Partridges
- Heron
- Quail
- Guinea Fowl
- Hawk

Calling on these animals can help you connect more deeply to Artemis, or noticing when they arrive in your life might be a sign of the goddess calling to you.

Though this is sometimes lost in the stories of Artemis, as the details of what She does tend to overshadow other beings, She is often described as having a hunting pack of hounds. These dogs are described in some hymns as

*two dogs black-and-white, three reddish, and one spotted.* Callimachus, Hymn 3 to Artemis 86 ff

They sometimes pull a golden chariot (or deer/stags do, depending on the story) to bring Artemis to the hunt.

## Herbs

Amaranth is a flower that connected Her to Amaranthus in Euboia, a place where one of Her many cults resided. This is a striking red flower. Asphodel is another herb for Artemis and is often used in animal feed. (Note: the roots are toxic.) In addition, this herb is connected with work in the underworld, so it is also associated with Hecate and Persephone.

Cypress is connected to the story of the birth of Apollo, as he was born in a place with cypress. And to be kept safe after his birth and the ire of Hera, Apollo was fed fruit and ambrosia. There is also a story of Apollo accidentally killing a deer of Cyparissus.[4] To make up for the accident, Apollo turned the deer into a tree, a cypress.

Another plant that comes from the birth story of Artemis and Apollo is the palm. Some translations describe Leto as giving birth while holding on to a palm tree on Delos.

When I think of Artemis, I think of Artemesia, or mugwort, the herb of dreaming and seeing. This herb was first named in the goddess' honor in 1753 by Carl Linnaeus.[5]

## Offerings

When thinking of ways to honor Artemis or any deity, I think about what I can offer to them. This means I think about what I have in my home first. Then I think about what I might seek to help honor this deity. Just like in dating or any relationship, I believe that gifts are kindness and don't have to be expensive or complicated.

Some offerings I suggest include:

- Naturally harvested antlers or fur
- Herbs: artemisia/mugwort, amaranth, asphodel, cypress, palm
- Water that's been blessed by moonlight
- Moon-shaped bread or cookies
- Arrows or spears (they don't have to be life-sized)
- Pictures or figurines of deer or other sacred animals
- Game meat or something of a hunt

When I drop into what a godds might want, I think about their movement in the worlds. What are they doing? What might they need in these journeys? This brings me to the hunt and what Artemis might want when She is hunting – or after She is hunting.

- What might restore Her?
- What might show Her of my hunting abilities?
- What might I give to Her that would help Her in the moonlight?

## Magickal Practice: What Can You Offer Artemis?

While physical items are a great way to connect with a deity, other offerings take less defined shapes. You might, for example, offer something of service to Artemis. This might be to care for animals or to care for those who need protection. The longer you work with a deity, the more you may want to give of yourself in other ways. In ways that interact with your life and what is important to you.

In thinking about how Artemis shows up and what She is associated with, can you drop into what might be important for you to do? In thinking about service and action, it is wise to consider what you already care about. For example, if you are already an animal lover, you might investigate ways to volunteer at shelters or sanctuaries.

If you are committed to nature and the wild, how can you help in your local area? Are there ways you can get involved to live a life that honors Artemis and Her wild?

While this is not a magickal practice that requires a candle or a chant, this is one of the most important practices for Artemis. She is not a deity of inaction. She engages in the world with Her fierceness and Her devotion. While She might make mistakes (and don't we all?), we can learn something from the boldness of this goddess.

I encourage you to act in some way. Whether this is a daily practice or a monthly trip to clean up trash along the road, find something that allows you to connect to the energy of Artemis. You might just hear from Her when you show up in this way. And if you're unsure of what to do, I encourage you to sit at Her altar and wait to see how inspiration might strike you. You might need to sit patiently before acting, much like a hunter waiting for the perfect time to aim.

# Chapter 7

# Devotional Practices

Martin Nilsson talked about how Artemis was of Minoan origin, known as the Mother Goddess in Asia Minor; "In those more distant times she was an older and ruder Artemis found in that wilderness of ragged peaks, deep forests, huge caves, and wet meadows. Her priestesses were wild women from the woods, half naked, savage, and orgiastic. We should not judge them as we would judge a civilized woman" (Goodrich 96-97)

Devotional work is one of the ways the godds are kept alive in modern times. While there are people who have documented ancient practices (as much as one can), I also believe the godds continue to live on with the introduction of modern practices.

To me, at least, there is no reason not to honor the godds with practices that make sense and are available to people today – and tomorrow. Plus, any relationship with a deity will expand and develop based on who is a part of that relationship. We bring ourselves to the godds as we are.

That said, it can help to take time to research what was going on in ancient Greece. Since these times were well-documented, you can find ways in which Artemis was previously celebrated and honored, which can inspire a modern version of honor.

## Cults of Artemis
To better learn about Artemis' worship and reverence, it helps to start with what was happening long before you and I have been alive.

Her cult flourished throughout the Mediterranean region during the Bronze Age. The Amazons built a beehive-shaped temple to Her at Ephesus circa 900 BC, and it is considered the Seventh Wonder of the ancient world. The temple contained a statue of Black Diana, on which was implanted a magical stone. Emperor Theodosius closed the temple in 380, allegedly because he despised the religion of women. Early Christians sought to destroy the cult as Devil-worshippers, and Black Diana was smashed circa 400 (Guiley 102).

It comes as no surprise to anyone, I imagine, that there were people who did not like Artemis and what She stood for. But Her worship was widespread, covering Northern, Southern, and Central Greece, Anatolia, the Aegean Sea, Italy, France, and Spain.

*[From a description of a painting depicting hunters:] Hunters as they advance will hymn Artemis Agrotera (Goddess of the Hunt); for yonder is a temple to her, and a statue worn smooth with age, and heads of boars and bears; and wild animals sacred to her graze there, fawns and wolves and hares, all tame and without fear of man. After a prayer the hunters continue the hunt.* Translated by Fairbanks. Philostratus the Elder, Imagines 1. 28

The temples would have statues and images of Artemis. Notable is the fact that the first stone temple built was to Artemis in Corcyra (Corfu). Previously, temples were made of wood, and using stone made them last longer (Garland 289). While these temples were not the only places one could worship Artemis or any other deity, they were places where devotees could witness sacrifices and rituals to Her.

These places might have been where children were birched for Artemis (Goodrich 365). This was a practice of using birch switches on children to help purify them. The birch was harvested in February and used in the springtime to align with the energy of resurrection and cleansing.

Men and women both were able to worship Artemis at the temple in Ephesus. And this temple helped support the needs of local women. "Aside from the temple of Artemis at Ephesus, where six thousand priestesses found useful employment, the greatest accumulations of such religious functionaries were probably employed by the queens of the ancient world" (Goodrich 375).

## Celebrations of Artemis

Like other Greek deities, there were special times when Artemis would be celebrated. While there were other festivals, the two that are often cited are Brauronia and Artemis Orthia.

### Brauronia

In the ritual of Brauronia, which happened every four years, worshippers would gather at Brauron to celebrate the transition from young girls (five to ten years of age) to first childbirth, as many girls in the ancient Greek world have children far earlier than we see today. Girls attending this rite would dance for Artemis, with the idea that Artemis was watching over them and initiating them into the mysteries of moving from girl to woman.

During the rite, offerings of spindles, and spindle whorls have been found, which likely indicates cloth and garments too. Girls in the ritual would take on the energy of bears, doing dances (arkteia) with specific steps and slow movements. As the girls moved in this ritual, they asked for the protection of Artemis and any advice Artemis might offer as they matured.

At one point, these rituals included bear skins for clothing, but later the girls wore saffron yellow dresses to symbolize the hard-to-find skins. Ultimately, the girls would remove their clothing to shed their old lives as they moved into womanhood.

## Artemis Orthia
In Sparta, Artemis Orthia was a sanctuary that held many celebrations, including a procession of girls, which seems to have a similar energy to Brauronia. This rite was a devotional practice, ensuring commitment to Artemis, with the girls singing and bringing offerings to the goddess.

## Laphria
Held in Patras, Laphria was a festival for Artemis that included the creation of a pyre and a procession to the goddess. A virgin priestess was the last to arrive at the pyre, riding in a chariot drawn by a deer. On the following day, there were sacrifices of birds, boars, deer, wolves, bears, and more, as well as fruit. The pyre was lit, and all was placed onto the altar.

## Mounykhia
In this festival of Artemis, it was customary to honor Her as the Lady of the Beasts and as a Moon goddess. A She-goat was dressed as a girl before being sacrificed. Round cakes with torches in the middle were brought to Artemis in a procession.

## Chants
While there are many ancient practices from which to draw inspiration, you might find you want to do other things and put your energy into this relationship with Artemis. Bringing your voice and energy to a godd is one of the many ways to honor them. You don't have to sing well or even have a specific song in mind, either. You can sing what comes to you or chant what

comes to you. These moments of your honest offering are gifts that connect and deepen the relationship.

Here are some chants you might want to use as part of your practice. You can find a tune that works for your voice. Or you can say the words aloud, repeating them until they fill the space.

### We Are the Wild Ones
We are the wild ones, and we are opening
We are the wild ones, and we are opening
Opening up to the wild, Artemis you call us
Irisanya Moon & River Roberts (2016)

### Silver Shining Wheel (partial lyrics)
Holy maiden huntress, Artemis, Artemis,
Maiden, come to us.
Silver shining wheel of radiance, radiance,
Mother, come to us.
Peter Soderberg (1987)

### Hunter Heart
Hunter, Huntress, Sovereign One
Help our aim be true
Hunter, Huntress, Sovereign One
Let us honor you
Irisanya Moon (2022)

When writing chants for Artemis, I might suggest one thing, namely, keep it simple. I think about the hunt and how it takes a lot of energy, keeping things simple makes more sense to me. But if your relationship with Artemis is more ritualistic and you find yourself in co-created temples with solemn rites, you might choose something more elaborate.

# Epithets

Sometimes calling out certain attributes of a godd can be helpful to empower a spell or to bring a sense of power to your body. You might choose to use these epithets after Artemis' name, repeating it, again and again to bring that power into the space and your heart.

Some of these epithets are those of other goddesses, used after their name to add power and precision. Other epithets are associated with the place where She was worshipped. While this is not an exhaustive list, it is meant to encourage you to see what happens when you focus on certain attributes of this huntress. See how they sound on your tongue and echo in your body.

**Agro'Tera** (Agrotera): the huntress
**Amarynthus** (Amarunthos): a hunter
**Apancho'Mene** (Apanchomenê): the strangled goddess
**Aristo** (Aristô): the best
**Aristobu'Le** (Aristobulê): the best adviser
**Chito'Ne** (Chitônê): huntress with Her chiton girt up
**Chrysaor** (Chrusaôr): golden sword or arms
**Coryphaea** (Koruphaia): the goddess who inhabits the summit of the mountain
**Game'Lii** (Gamêlioi theoi): protecting and presiding over marriage
**Genetyllis** (Genetullis): protectress of births
**Hege'Mone** (Hêgemonê): leader or ruler
**Hemere'Sia** (Hêmerêsia): soothing goddess
**Heurippe** (Heurippa): finder of horses
**Lime'Nia**, **Limeni'Tes**, **Limeni'Tis**, and **Limeno'Scopus** (Limenia, Limenitês, Limenitis, Limenodkopos): protector or superintendent of the harbor

**Limnaea, Limne'Tes, Limne'Genes** (Limnaia os, Limnêtês is, Limnêgenês): inhabiting or born in a lake or marsh
**Locheia** (Locheia): protectress of women in childbed
**Lysizo'Na** (Lusizônê): the goddess who loosens the girdle
**Melissa** (Melissa): goddess of the moon, alleviating the suffering of women in childbirth
**O'Rthia** (Orthia, Orthias, or Orthôsia): goddess of the moon
**Parthe'Nia** (Parthenia): maiden
**Peitho** (Peithô): persuasion
**Phoebe** (Phoibê): goddess of the moon
**Pho'Sphorus** (Phôsphoros): goddess of light
**Soteira** (Sôteira): the saving goddess
**Upis** (Oupis): assisting women in childbirth

A practice I have been trying to cultivate with more vigor involves learning Greek pronunciations. Now, as one of my Greek friends has told me, there are many ways to pronounce these words, including ancient, modern, and location-based ways. What I try to do is to look up the pronunciations and try them out. When I find something that feels right, I try to say that again and again. I try to tap into the feeling that comes from using my voice in a certain way, in a way that many others may have done for centuries. This helps me get more connected and more engaged in a practice that feels respectful.

## Magickal Practice: Hunting with Artemis
To hunt with Artemis is to take on a sacred task. This powerful work will help you step into your sense of wild-heartedness. I recommend this practice when you are feeling powerless or when you feel you don't know or recognize what power you have.

I encourage you to do this practice with another person or persons whenever possible. It will help you have a more embodied experience. With more than one of you, you can step into the hunt more easily and notice what happens in relation to another living being.

But if this is not possible, you can still do this. I'll give instructions for both.

## With Others

Gather in a space that is safe for you to gather. This might be a room, but it could also be an outdoor space where you can move around without being bothered.

Take a moment to think about Artemis. Think about what She looks like in your mind, how She already shows up in your life, or how She might start to show up in your life. Start to pull up energy from the earth below you, allowing that energy to start to infuse you with the wild. Notice how your body starts to feel and how it starts to move when you call the wild into yourself.

As part of this wildness, this conjuring of nature, start to think about how Artemis travels in these spaces. What do Her legs do? How does She move Her arms? You can do all of this with your eyes open or closed. Allow Her energy to fill you and to allow you to understand what it means to be a goddess of the hunt.

Once you feel Her and the nature of wild things in your body, you can open your eyes if they have been closed. Start to move around the space in this body that is now more alive and wilder. Notice how you interact with the room or nature around you. Notice how you interact with others:

- Do you look them in the eye?
- Do you feel differently about them?
- Do you want to yell or scream?
- Do you want to move faster?
- Do you want to run?

Start to think about the hunt and how you might join the hunt with Her. This part will look different for everyone, but it often looks like everyone is chasing each other until they are tired. If you want to add some intensity, you can find a playlist and run with the sound of drums or some other deep rhythm. Step into the movement of the hunt and see how it makes your body, mind, and heart feel.

You can hunt for as long as you like, for as long as you want. Some will do this until they are exhausted and can't move anymore. You don't have to go that far. You can move until it feels right to stop. And when you do stop, I encourage you to lie on the floor or ground and let any excess energy drop into the earth. Give the extra energy back to the earth to compost and to be nourished.

For groups where movement might be limited or inaccessible, you can lie down in a circle with your heads in the middle. From there, you can say aloud what you see and what you feel, with voices layering on each other to feed the working. Once the conversation dies down, you can close things up and move back into the space, sitting up to transition into the present day.

It can help to write down any experiences you had, even if they don't make sense. They might make sense in a few days, or they might later offer you insight into what action you need to take next. In a group, you might decide to share the details of your experience or not.

### On Your Own

After reading the section on this practice in a group, you may already have a good idea about how to move your body to join the hunt. If you haven't read the section, here are some ideas.

Start with a place where you feel safe in your body and mind. This might be your room or another room where you live. It might be in a natural setting that is comfortable for you and where you won't be disturbed.

This practice can also be done lying down and as a completely internal process. You don't have to move your body unless that feels good to you. However you like to prepare before magickal work, do that first. You might put on a special outfit, or you might light incense, or you might look at your Artemis altar. Come into a place in your body that is grounded and sacred.

Once you are settled and ready, drop your awareness into the floor beneath you and the earth beneath you. Tap into the energy of the wild, the roots, the places of composting and growth. Tap in and begin to pull that energy and inspiration into your body. When you feel this is complete and ready, start to call Artemis in the way that makes the most sense to you. You might invite Her to the hunt, you might call Her name. You might make a sound. Whatever feels right.

Call Her. Once you feel She is present, move your body in any way that feels good. It can help to have instrumental and drum-led music in the background. You might move with this music, allowing your limbs to sway as they fill up with the energy of the hunt and the goddess.

It might feel good to move your body as a huntress. To move your awareness and mind into the places of chase and action. This might mean you chase yourself around the room, or you travel in your mind to a place where you can run for miles. Travel through space and time and possibility:

- What does it feel like to hunt?
- What are you chasing?
- Who are you chasing?
- How can you capture what you want to capture?
- How will you know this is a successful hunt?

This is a practice of becoming present in what happens at this moment. A hunt may not end up the way you envisioned it at the start. You may start by hunting one thing but realize you need to hunt for something completely different. You might find something you need.

Allow yourself to be a part of the hunt for as long as it makes sense to you. This might be a minute, and it might be more. But once you are done, return to your body, dropping to the floor or ground to let any excess energy be released back to the kind earth.

Rest there until you feel ready to come back to the present moment. Feel free to journal about what you noticed, found, and learned.

# Chapter 8

# Cultivating a Relationship with the Wild

How does one start to build a relationship with that which changes each day?
How do you come into a relationship with what you have always been?
How do you return to the places of authenticity?
How do you call back your power and the bow of your intention?
How do you join the hunt for your own heart again?

I don't have all the answers to these questions, but Artemis does. She knows what it takes to come back into your being. To come back to the wild from which you have been born and created and made. To come back to the sacred hunt that needs you and knows you.

To take up the bow and the tools of protection.
To take up the skills of tending birth and death.
To take up the promises of watching over those you love.
To live by the moon and the power of ritual.
To come back into your full being, without shame or hesitation.

There is no time for hesitation in this hunt.

## How to Relate to a Godd

Building a relationship with a godd, like any relationship, takes time. It takes commitment and a willingness to show up when things are hard. Because the godds seem so different from us, it can be confusing to start. But what I would offer is that you already know how to build relationships with humans, and that is a great place to begin.

I offer a few guidelines before beginning:

1. Know your intention
2. Trust the process
3. Be present and patient
4. Recognize when it is and isn't working
5. Show up because you want to be there, not because you want something

Let's walk through this list together.

### Know your intention

While I have gone into relationships that didn't seem to have a goal or an intention, working with the godds is another process. Though I hold to the idea that working with the godds is very similar to humans, it also does include more devotion and intentionality. (I don't have altars for my friends, after all.)

You might start, as you did earlier in this book, with an idea about what you want from working with Artemis. Or you might find signs that lead you to believe She wants to work with you. In either case, it helps to get clear.

What do you want to work on?
Why do you want to work together?
Do you have a goal?
What kind of relationship might this be?

For the last question, think about whether this is a short-term relationship or if you want something a bit more formal and long-lasting. This doesn't mean you can't change your mind later, but it is smart to think about what you want now, as that will set the stage for how you interact.

## Trust the process

Of course, it would be great to know how things are going to go and how things are going to turn out in any relationship. When we begin with a friendship or a romantic relationship, we hope things are easy and simple. But this is not the way of humans, and it's certainly not the way of humans working with godds. (At least not for me.)

At first, there needs to be a certain level of trust in yourself and the godd. You might approach Artemis as someone you want to learn from and someone you want to have help you. But just because these are things you know, it does not mean they will look the way you think they will look. For example, learning about your strength from Artemis might mean you encounter a bunch of scenarios where you will learn how strong you are. And those are not always desirable, expected, or fun. But they are teaching you, and trusting the process can help to allow the lessons to work on you.

## Be present and patient

Along with trusting, it helps to enter these relationships with patience and presence. Show up when you say you will show up and recognize not everything works on the timeline you might want. Often, I will hear folks talk about how a deity is not responding in the timeframe they expected. Or that things aren't changing as fast as they would like.

Such is the way of working with godds whose concept of time differs from humans. Imagine being able to see all things and all times at once, and someone is asking you to hurry up. It's not the best exchange of energy. (And humans are the same way. Imagine wanting your friends to do things on your timeline all the time. Does that sound realistic? Does that sound reasonable?)

Instead, allow yourself to sink into the process with presence and patience. Let things happen in the time they do. If you feel things are taking 'too long,' then check in with yourself to see if you are holding up your end of the relationship. If not, then maybe it's time to consider what more you could be doing.

### Recognize when it is and isn't working

It's also possible that things might not work with you and this deity. You might have a clear agreement, you might do everything you've promised, and you may not feel good about this partnership. You don't have to stay. You can decide things aren't working, thank the godd for their time, and move on.

Like any relationship, if it's not working for one of you, it's probably not working for both of you. Again, check in with yourself about whether you have given the attention you need to give, and if so, you might start to consider if you need to step back or step away completely.

### Show up because you want to be there, not because you want something

One of the most human things to do in a relationship is to expect your actions to lead to certain outcomes. If I am nice to you, you are nice to me. If I give you a gift, you will give me a gift.

More often than not, this is what happens. We teach others how to treat us by how we treat them. But this doesn't always mean that this is appropriate or should be expected. Instead, it is wise to show up because you want the relationship to work, not because you only want a certain outcome.

What if the outcome is something better than what you've asked for? Will you be upset because you didn't get what you gave? As with any relationship, check in with your motives. When you do, you will often find the answer to any tension or confusion about what is (or is not) happening.

## Hunting with Artemis

To hunt with Artemis is to find yourself in a place of possibility and patience. To hunt with Her (and anyone) is to come with the best tools and training and know you might not get what you came for. For me, this is a practice of living in the world, and it is a practice that is vital.

On the one hand, some people will find it helpful to learn to hunt animals and provide food for themselves. This can be not only helpful in living one's life close to nature but also helpful in connecting more deeply to this huntress goddess. But it's not feasible or palatable for everyone.

It would seem that the goddess who personifies the wildness of nature evokes the most primitive fear of dependence on forces that are beyond the control of human beings, and whose law they can, therefore, violate without knowing it (Baring & Cashford 327).

This relationship with the wild is complicated and, often, our impact is unknown. This can conjure up hard feelings that can leave you feeling stifled and stuck. But to be a hunter is to know how to move through these moments and aim well.

## Sitting with Fear

With the guidance and blessing of Artemis, I encourage you to contemplate what fear means to you. I am hopeful you do not live in fear daily, and I hope you are in a space that is safe for you to breathe and be in. And even if this is true, fear arrives when it does. It comes to the table, to the bedroom, to the conversations, and to the moments in which we wish we could think clearly.

I invite you to sit in a space that calls Artemis to sit by your side. This might be at an altar or in a wild space. This might be somewhere else. I invite you to find yourself in a space where you can relax and return to a sense of safety. One of my favorite practices is becoming more aware of my body and its place at the moment. This can be done with eyes open or closed.

You can do this by allowing your attention to arrive at different body parts. You might start with your toes and your ankles. There is nothing special to do but pay attention to how they feel. This is a practice of noticing, not fixing.

Then you can travel up your body, along your calves and thighs. Travel the space of your hips and pelvic bowl. Move and linger in the space of your stomach and along each rib and vertebrae. Find yourself paying attention to your heart and lungs. Arrive along the stretch of your arms, from shoulder to elbow, to fingertips and thumbs.

Move back to the space of your collarbone and neck and up to your jaw. This might be a place of tension, so you can notice this and invite the possibility that it can release if it wants to. And then, notice the temperature of your skin and any sensations in your face and forehead before moving to the of your head. When you have taken time to think about your body and its parts, notice where you are. If your eyes are closed, open them. Without moving your body, let your eyes travel the space around you. See that you are safe and secure. Recognize that you are surrounded by things you know. Once you are in this space, make sure you feel safe and present. If there is anything else you need to do, please do that now.

For just a moment or two, I invite you to drop into yourself. Notice that in your mind is a space where you are called to, a place where you are meant to be right now. This space is calm and quiet. It feels right, and it feels like it has something to teach you. You might notice or feel the presence of Artemis. Or you might notice it is wild and wonderful.

As you are there, you can sit down or rest in a way that works for you and your body. Once you are there, notice that a screen or clear space opens up. It starts to show you scenes of your life.

Even if you can't see things clearly, you begin to feel them and notice how they are telling you stories of yourself. Even if you can't see this, you can feel what is happening and you easily travel back to these life scenes.

With a breath, you notice the scenes shift to something that causes you to feel fear. This does not need to be the deepest trauma of your life, and right now, it should be simple, perhaps something you fear without knowing why.

You begin to see this thing or situation in front of you, or you feel it arrive. At this moment, it is separate from you. It is not a part of you, and you can turn away from the screen or space at any time if it's not the work you need to do today.

As you sit in this space, allow your body to tell you what it feels. It might tell you about fear through shallow breath or a faster heartbeat. It might tell you by a change in your temperature or a sinking feeling in your stomach. Notice where the fear arrives in your unique body.

Once you notice the feeling, just be with it. There is no need to tell a story about it or try to explain why you feel this way. You just do. It is not wrong or bad. It is fear. It is a way that you feel in response to something. If it helps, take a breath or shake your body, or move. Sit with this fear for about 90 seconds. You don't have to time it, but you also can.

Remember, the invitation is to sit in the feeling for a little bit. Once you have sat for about 90 seconds, let this fear go. You can tear down the screen or turn away. Or do something else that tells your body you are done with this exercise.

At this moment, sit with how your body feels. What does it feel like after sitting alongside fear for a little while? There are no wrong answers. What is right for you is what is right for you. And when you feel ready, you can begin to open your eyes and come back to the room you are in. Again, look at the space around you, know you are safe and sound. Some find it helpful to journal about what they felt.

This practice is one to return to now and again. The more you can sit with fear, the more you can sit with uncomfortable emotions. The research says that when you do this, you can process the feeling because you are letting it arrive without judgment or tension.

Now, you may not feel this is what happened to you today. That's okay. It's a practice. You can sit with Artemis to find out what you might need to know, and you might need to adjust things to see what might work better the next time.

Once you can sit with discomfort and allow it to sit beside you, you will be able to hunt what you truly want in your life. You can hold discomfort and excitement or any number of emotions simultaneously. All are feelings. And all can be welcome. When we can hold these feelings, we can aim without shaking or hesitation.

## The Navigation of Uncertainty

The world is filled with moments we cannot predict. These lives are filled with opportunities to grow and expand our experience. But this is often laced with times of uncertainty. How do we move forward if we aren't sure things will work out? How do we keep going (whatever that means to you) if there is no certain outcome?

It's hard work. And it's the modern version of the hunt. We can have everything in place, we can know the things we need to know, and we can still not get what we want. Uncertainty has caused me to hesitate, often holding myself back because that seemed easier than failing. But I also know this has made me miss out on things.

One of the practices I turn to when I am unsure and uncertain is to travel back in my life to times that felt like this. I travel back to places I have been and the decisions I made. I sometimes close my eyes and go back to 'past me' to see what I was thinking and what happened. I remind myself that things always resolve in some way. Now, this doesn't mean that everything always works out how I want it to (that would be so nice if that were always the case).

But what it does offer is the chance to prove to myself that I have felt this way before. And I will feel this way again. Hundreds of times, millions of times – if I'm lucky to live that long.

Another practice to navigate uncertainty is to follow the moon. It can help to have a practice of acknowledging the changes of the moon and the way they will shift toward newness or fullness, no matter what you do. No matter what anyone does. While there are things that will always be uncertain, there are some things in nature you can be certain of.

Think about seasons, the cycle of seed to plant to compost, the movement of water from rain to the river to ocean, and the travel of light across a day.

When uncertain, you can also look to the skies and the plants. You can look at the way the world moves. You can become present in the right now. To the places that are often easy to miss or forget or overlook. When you are on the hunt, you need to notice these things too, because they can point to how things might turn out.

For example, if you feel like everything in your life is slow or stuck, look to the moon. Is it growing? If so, you might look at your life for examples of how things are growing. And if you can't find that, what could you start to grow, if only with one little note of encouragement on a piece of paper? And if the moon is waning to new, can you consider the possibility that maybe this is just a moment in your life when you're supposed to rest and slow down?

When uncertain, you can dance with nature and follow the spiral staircase of possibility that is living in this world. It spins, turns on itself, and we find ourselves in familiar places but with more wisdom than before. I promise.

## Redefining Success

If the object of the hunt for Artemis (and any hunter) is to kill an animal, then that can be seen as the only marker of success. That makes sense in this capitalistic world: we must produce to have value and worth. We must keep doing and doing and getting better all the time. But is this true? Or is it something that we've been taught to keep us working?

I think about this often and am actively trying to dismantle that thinking, to come back to the place that is me. To come back to the person that I am and want to continue to be. This requires I get honest and clear about what I think success is. (Hint: it changes a lot for me.)

Can I see success in the way I love? In the people around me?
Can I measure success by how many moments I can be present for what is happening?
Can I feel successful when my body asks me to rest, and I rest?
Can I know success in saying no to what I don't want?
Can I claim success when I achieve the smallest goal?
Can I accept that I am successful when I have done what I needed to do to survive?

Success does not need to be measured in numbers. It does not need to be measured in the likes and hearts on social media. It does not need to be counted alongside a bank account or investments. It can be a practice of attention to what is important for you to do and feel.

The measure of success can be a feeling of knowing your skin. Of knowing what is best for you -– without the opinion of another. I can't imagine Artemis asking others for their opinions of what She should do or how She should act. She asked Zeus for what She wanted because it's what She wanted.

You don't need to explain your measure of success to anyone. You can be the person who defines success by the people they love or the creatures that cuddle up by their feel each night. You get to define this.

So, define it. You can write this down, but if you want a more embodied practice, I encourage you to move your body to music or the sounds of nature. And as you do, think about what success could mean. Allow the feeling that lets you know success has arrived, let that feeling move you and whisper to you. Picture what it feels like, smells like, and tastes like. Allow it to fill up your heartbeat and your lungs. Get to know that feeling. And every time you need to check if you're doing something that will make you feel successful, see if that feeling is present. If that feeling isn't there, you might need to reevaluate your actions and your plans.

How exciting.

## Calling to Artemis

No matter the deity I work with, I tend to write things and call them with poems and other writings. This helps me ground sacred words into my body, and I think of those words as gifts that I extend to divine beings. (I also think deities like to hear their name a lot.)

You can choose to write your own or use some of the quotes in this book, as well as this translation of the Homeric Hymn to Artemis. (There was another translation earlier in the book, so you have options.)

*Artemis I sing*
*with her golden arrows*
*and her hunting cry*
*the sacred maiden*
*deer-huntress*

*showering arrows*
*sister of Apollo*
*with his golden sword*

*In mountains of shadow*
*and peaks of wind*
*She delights in the chase,*
*she arches her bow*
*of solid gold*

*She lets fly*
*arrows*
*that moan*

*Crests*
*of high mountains*
*tremble,*
*the forest*
*in darkness*
*screams*
*with the terrible howling*
*of wild animals*

*the earth itself shudders,*
*even the sea*
*alive with fish*

*But the heart of the goddess*
*is strong,*
*she darts everywhere*
*in and out, every way*
*killing*
*the race of beasts.*

*And when she has had enough*
*of looking for animals,*
*this huntress*
*who takes pleasure in arrows,*
*when her heart is elated,*
*then she unstrings*
*her curved bow*

*and goes*
*to the great house*
*of Phoebus Apollo,*
*her dear bother,*
*in the fertile grasslands*
*of Delphi*
*and there she arranges*
*the lovely dances*
*of the Muses and Graces*

*There she hangs up*
*Her unstrung bow*
*and her quiver of arrows,*
*and gracefully*
*clothing her body*
*She takes first place*
*at the dances*
*and begins*

*With heavenly voices*
*they all sing*

*they sing of Leto*
*with her lovely ankles,*
*how she gave birth*

*to the best children*
*of all the gods,*
*supreme*
*in what they say*
*and do.*

*Farewell*
*children of Zeus and Leto,*
*She of the beautiful hair.*
*Now*
*and in another song*
*I will remember you.*

Translated by Jules Cashford. Homeric Hymns

If you and I were doing a ritual together, we might read sections of this translation aloud. We would call to each other with the words of this hymn. And when we were done, we might call out words or phrases that impacted us or new words we wanted to offer to Artemis so that She might feel celebrated.

There is no reason why you can't write a new Artemis hymn. Or find another way to share the same ideas in dance or movement, or art. All of these things can call to the goddess. I would also encourage you to find these hymns in Greek. Hearing the hymns in this language offers another wholly holy experience. And you might even be inspired to call out Her name in Greek.

Ἄρτεμις, which sounds to me like AR-ta-mees. There are modern and ancient Greek languages, so you might find another pronunciation. Say them all aloud to see what rings through your bones.

## Altars for Artemis

In a previous chapter, we talked about the different creatures and herbs associated with Artemis, as well as some of the things that you might offer to Her. Let's expand on that so you can create a special space for Her in your life.

I believe altars allow for a more intentional connection with the godds. In these spaces, we can have a place just for the work between the two of you. This altar will become stronger as you sit with it and devote energy to it. It will change and evolve as your relationship grows.

For Artemis, I encourage you to start with something simple. After all, She is the goddess of the hunt. To me, this means that She is not going to be too fancy in the way She carries herself and how She wants to be honored. Now, it is clear She does want to be honored, but I don't think She needs to have anything too complicated. (But it's your relationship with Her, you might learn and do otherwise.)

A simple altar might be a piece of nature that you have on a table or desk or windowsill. It might be something you visit every day or add new things to as inspiration strikes. On my altar to Artemis, I have a small statue of Her. And when I'm working with Her more deliberately, I have a naturally shed deer antler beside Her, as well as a small offering bowl. That bowl will hold anything I might find for Her.

Over time, altars will change and grow and often move to new places. I like to have altars that are close to windows so they can get some sunlight and moonlight on them at different parts of the day. You might choose to have an altar outside for Artemis, as that seems to be where She typically is.

I would also encourage you to place altars in nature. This might happen as you're walking in a forest and seeing something Artemis might like. (Something natural, please, and biodegradable, of course). You might take a moment to let Her know you are leaving this for Her and then set it down as an offering for Her along Her hunt.

Of course, you can have more complicated altars for Her. I truly believe the godds like to have special places for themselves. But you can also create an altar that changes with the seasons. It doesn't have to be stagnant. You can also change the altar to suit what you are working on now.

Maybe the altar for Artemis is about birthright now. And maybe later, you might focus on healing or hunting. If there's anything that Artemis is known for, it's adaptability and intuition. Check in with what you feel is right and see how it feels as you continue communicating with Her.

## Magickal Practice: Tapping into Instinct

Can you trust yourself when things are difficult? Can you tap into what is true for you when it matters? Are you out of touch with your instinctual nature? If you said yes to any of these questions, you're not alone.

Like any relationship, it is natural to fall in and out of a relationship with yourself and with your instincts. It's easy when we are in a world that wants us to be disconnected from our bodies. It is common because the word asks us to only use logic to solve problems. But not all questions can be answered that easily. We need to tap back into our bodies.

I think of the way a hunter must trust in their body to know when to be quiet, when to turn a certain way, and when to shoot the arrow. While you may not be hunting, you can tap back into your instincts.

*(Note: sometimes tapping into our instinct or intuition is harder if we have trauma or a history of traumatic events. Please know you can step into this as much as feels good and no more. You are in control of what you choose to do.)*

There are two practices I'd like you to try.

## Notice What You Know

The first practice is simple but powerful. Each day, I want you to wake up and tell yourself that you will trust your instincts. You don't have to believe this. All you have to do is to say this. You might feel like touching a part of your body when you say this. Or not. You might hold your heart as you say this.

Go to a quiet place and journal what your instincts told you about certain events, interactions, and conversations at the end of your day. Even if you didn't act on what you felt, think about when you felt certain things or hits of insight. Write these down. Start to notice how your body feels when these hits happen. I notice my heart gets a little quicker when I feel something is happening or my ears ring.

Once you have the hang of this, you can move into acting on your intuition and writing about that. What happened? How did things go? You might have moments when you don't interpret things correctly, and that's okay. You are learning and re-learning. It takes practice.

You can choose the time period for this practice, but I find 30 days is a great container as it is long enough to see results and long enough to notice what your body tells you.

## Take Up the Bow

As a more advanced practice, I offer a lighter form of aspecting. This is a practice that I learned in Reclaiming Witchcraft as a form of possessory work. This is a practice of calling deity energy into your body so that a godd might use your body to move and communicate. I recommend practicing aspecting in groups first before doing this on your own, but this exercise will be a lighter version of what is often done. This version will be asking you to aspect yourself from another time.

In this practice, I encourage you to take a breath to calm yourself. Picture in your mind and heart a specific time when you felt connected with the world. You could understand the energies that were speaking to you, that were telling you what you need to know. Your heart was clear and true.

Call that feeling into your body, allowing it to push aside any sense of doubt or worry. Let it push the everyday way and beyond. You can pick up the ordinary later. But for now, allow your body and mind to be filled with confidence and true nature. Take up the bow of instinct and courage. You know what to do. You know the next right step.

You might choose to move your body and see how it feels to move in the world with this energy. You might look at nature and see if it looks different. You might interact with an animal or a human to see how things feel. They don't need to know, but they might figure out that you're in a different space.

When you have filled up every corner of your body with this experience, find a place on your body where you can anchor this experience. Anchoring can look like touching your heart and placing the energy or wisdom of an experience there. When the experience is rooted in your body, if you need that experience again, you can just touch that place and return to the feeling.

As you feel ready to release this feeling, you might take a deep breath and release it from your body. You might clap or move out of the space you are in to change it up. You might fill yourself with how you felt before, though it might feel different now.

You can call your instinct back into yourself. It never left. But the more you call it back, the louder it will become, and the more it will be a part of your everyday experience.

## Magickal Practice: Dedication to Artemis

I've left this section for the end because I don't think it's a small matter to dedicate yourself to a godd. I think it's a decision that is best thought through and considered. While I also don't think that dedication means you are connected for life, this is not something to do unless you are okay with it being a lifelong commitment. But you do what works for you.

## Ideal Timing & Location:

New moon (or three days before or after)
Nature space (but your room or house is fine too)

## Items You Need:

Candle
Altar items:

- Something to hold the energy of the wild, e.g., a branch, a leaf, an herb sacred to Artemis, etc.
- Water from a local source, and if not available, your tap water will do
- Something to signify a bow and arrow, or an actual bow and arrow – don't worry about the size
- A figure or picture of Artemis

## Preparation:

Cleanse your body before this rite
Create an altar for Artemis
Write down your promises to Her

## Ritual:

Begin with acknowledging the land you are on, especially if you are on colonized land
Create sacred space, e.g., grounding, casting, elemental invocations, etc.

Call Artemis and invite Her into the space and light the candle

Sit in the sacred space, looking at the altar and the image of Artemis. Allow your eyes to soften and to close if you like. Drop into a wild space waiting for you that might be in light or complete darkness, showing the slightest sliver of the new moon's arrival or departure. Sink into this space and wait for Artemis to join you. This might take seconds, and it might take longer. Ready yourself for whatever comes next.

(If She does not arrive, it might be wise to wait for another day to do this rite. You can close the circle and thank Artemis for Her time.)

When She arrives, either in form or feeling, notice what She is doing and what She has for you. This might reveal itself loudly, or it might be gentle and subtle. If She does not offer you anything, you can ask Her to listen to your request. From there, you request that you be in service to Her and dedicated to Her for some period of time, or forever. When you do this, you might wait to see what She says, or you can move to read the list of things you promise to do for Her during this connection.

(Know this process is not one to be rushed. Hunts are not to be rushed. Sit and be patient for whatever might happen. Know that this outline might change in the moment. Be ready and willing to do what needs to be done.)

After you have read your promises, sit and receive what comes next. This might be loud or subtle, as it is just for you and not something that can be predicted.

If you feel that things have been accepted and heard by Artemis, you can choose to anoint yourself with water by using a leaf or branch or another piece of nature. You might hold the natural item on top of your heart, even lying down to rest with the earth, and let the ground hold you in this sacred moment.

Allow yourself to be there as long as you like. Notice whatever happens and what you might be called to do. When you feel you have stepped into the fullness of your promise to Artemis, I encourage you to stand up and face Her.

Say something like: *I am ready to hunt with you.*

When you feel this has landed in your bones and bow, thank Artemis. Thank Her for this new connection and relationship. Devoke and open the circle. Leave the candle burning for a little while, and then put the flame out. Return to the candle for strength and the moments when you might need some extra energy from Her.

# Conclusion

*Artemis of Wild Places and Wild Spaces*
*Goddess of the Wide Open, Wild Open Hearts*
*We call to you*
*We ask that we might join you in the forests of possibility*
*In the dense places where finding our footing is crucial*
*In the chases where trusting our aim is essential*
*We call to you*
*Bless us with your confidence and your knowing*
*Bless us with your strength and direction*
*Bless us with the wisdom to know when to pick up the bow*
*And when to put it down*
*Artemis, Wild One, Sovereign One*
*You who is hard to see in the night*
*But known by moonlight*
*We honor you and call to you when it's time to run in the direction*
*of our own power*
–Irisanya Moon

Artemis is calling to many of us. She has been calling us back to the wild, back to the places where we are one with nature, where we are willing to sacrifice that which does not support us, and where we can be truly free unto ourselves.

No matter how you identify, no matter where you have arrived in your life right now, Artemis offers the wisdom of truth and the strength of discernment. She asks you to know what you want and to ask for it, to demand it. She ask you to step fully into your power.

In these times that contain ongoing overwhelm and worry, Artemis offers you the strength you need to keep moving forward, knowing your wild and sovereign heart.

In times when you are powerful and sure, Artemis offers you companionship and protection, the kind of allyship that requires devotion and reciprocity.

And it is worth it.
*Hail Artemis.*

# Brief Glossary

Here is a short listing of godds, places, and events mentioned in this book to help you get a sense of who they are and how they relate to each other.

**Aphrodite** – goddess of love and beauty, daughter of Zeus and Dione.

**Apollo** – brother of Artemis, god of archery, music, prophecy, healing, and more.

**Artemis** – daughter of Leto and Zeus, goddess of the hunt, women and childbirth, and animals.

**Athena** – born fully formed from the forehead of Zeus, goddess of war and discipline.

**Demeter** – goddess of agriculture, sister of Zeus and Hera, mother of Persephone.

**Eleusinian Mysteries** – annual initiations held for the cult of Demeter and Persephone.

**Hades** – son of Chronos and Rhea, god of the dead and king of the underworld.

**Hecate** – daughter of Perses and Asteria, goddess of crossroads, magick, earth, sea, and sky.

**Hera** – goddess of marriage, women, and family, daughter of Kronos and Rhea.

**Nymphs** – minor nature deities.

**Olympians** – major Greek deities: Zeus, Poseidon, Hera, Demeter, Aphrodite, Athena, Artemis, Apollo, Ares, Hephaestus, Hermes, and Dionysus (sometimes Hestia).

**Orion** – giant hunter who hunted with Artemis, placed into the sky by Artemis or Zeus as stars.

**Persephone** – goddess of the seasons, daughter of Demeter, travels to the underworld either by choice or force, depending on the story.

**Titans** – pre-Olympian gods, Oceanus, Tethys, Hyperion, Theia, Coeus, Phoebe, Kronus, Rhea, Mnemosyne, Themis, Crius, and Iapetus.

**Trojan War** – war waged in the city of Troy by the Achaeans when Paris of Troy took Helen from Her husband Menelaus, king of Sparta.

**Underworld** – known as the House of Hades, containing the River Styx, amongst other rivers, where souls of those who have died return.

**Zeus** – god of the sky, son of Kronos/Cronos and Rhea and grandson of Earth and Heaven.

# End Notes

1. https://www.tni.org/en/publication/a-land-sovereignty-alternative-0#:~:text=Land%20sovereignty%20is%20the%20right,resource%2C%20territory%2C%20and%20landscape
2. https://www.mossyoak.com/our-obsession/blogs/cuzs-corner/the-effect-moon-phase-has-on-hunting-deer
3. Strabo. ed. H. L. Jones, The Geography of Strabo
4. https://8billiontrees.com/trees/types-of-cypress-trees/#:~:text=It%20is%20believed%20that%20the,the%20Cypress%20tree%20was%20born
5. https://en.wikipedia.org/wiki/Artemisia_(plant)

# Appendix

## Additional Resources

Graves, Robert. *The Greek Myths.*

Hamilton, Edith. *Mythology.*

Homer. *Iliad.*

Homer. *Odyssey.*

Mankey, Jason and Taylor, Astrea. *Modern Witchcraft with the Greek Gods: History, Insights & Magickal Practice.*

West, M.L. *Hesiod: Theogony and Works and Days.*

# Bibliography

## Books

Baring, Anne and Cashford, Jules. *The Myth of the Goddess: Evolution of an Image.*

Bolen, Jean Shinoda. *Goddesses in Everywoman: Powerful Archetypes in Women's Lives.*

Burkert, Walter. *Greek Religion.*

Cashford, Julies. *Homeric Hymns.*

Connelly, Joan Breton. *Portrait of a Priestess: Women and Ritual in Ancient Greece.*

D'Este, Sorita. *Artemis: Virgin Goddess of the Sun & Moon.*

Euripides. *Hippolytus.*

Evelyn-White, Hugh G. (English translator). *The Homeric Hymns and Homerica.*

Fantham, Elaine; Peet Foley, Helene; Boymel Kampden, Natalie; Pomeroy, Sarah B.; and Shapiro, H. Alan. *Women in the Classical World.*

Garland, Robert. *Daily Life of the Ancient Greeks, Second Edition.*

Goodrich, Norma Lorre. *Priestesses.*

Graziosi, Barbara. *The Gods of Olympus.*

Guiley, Rosemary Guiley. *The Encyclopedia of Witches and Witchcraft.*

Lefkowitz, Mary R. *Women in Greek Myth.*

Malamud, Rene. *The Amazon Problem.*

Monaghan, Patricia. *The New Book of Goddesses & Heroines.*

Paris, Ginette. *Pagan Mediations: The Worlds of Aphrodite, Artemis, and Hestia.*

Pomeroy, Sarah B. *Goddesses, Whores, Wives, and Slaves: Women in Classical Antiquity.*

Spretnak, Charlene. *Lost Goddesses of Early Greece: A Collection of Pre-Hellenic Myths.*

Strabo. *The Geography of Strabo.*

Trzaskoma, Stephen M.; Smith, R. Scott; and Brunet, Stephen (edited and translated by). *Anthology of Classical Myth: Primary Sources in Translation, Second Edition.*

Weigle, Marta. *Spiders and Spinsters: Women and Mythology.*

## Websites

https://www.britannica.com/topic/Artemis-Greek-goddess

https://en.wikipedia.org/wiki/Artemis

https://en.wikipedia.org/wiki/Cult_of_Artemis_at_Brauron

https://en.wikipedia.org/wiki/Laphria_(festival)

https://en.wikipedia.org/wiki/Sanctuary_of_Artemis_Orthia

https://exploringyourmind.com/the-myth-of-artemis-goddess-of-nature/

https://www.forerunner.com/champion/X0001_Birthing_Abortion

https://greekgodsandgoddesses.net/goddesses/artemis/

https://www.greekmythology.com/Olympians/Artemis/artemis.html

https://www.hellenion.org/festivals/mounykhia/

https://kosmossociety.chs.harvard.edu/artemis-pourer-of-arrows/

https://www.theoi.com/Olympios/Artemis.html

https://www.worldhistory.org/artemis/

# About the Author

Irisanya Moon is a priestess and teacher who teaches classes and camps worldwide, including in the US, Canada, UK, and Australia. She was initiated into the Reclaiming Witchcraft tradition in 2014. She blogs at *Patheos – Charged by the Goddess* and is a regular contributor to *Pagan Dawn*. You can find out more at www.irisanyamoon.com.

Books by Irisanya Moon
*Pagan Portals: Reclaiming Witchcraft*
*Pagan Portals: Aphrodite – Encountering the Goddess of Love & Beauty & Initiation*
*Pagan Portals: Iris – Goddess of the Rainbow & Messenger of the Godds*
*Pagan Portals: The Norns – Weavers of Fate & Magick*

*Practically Pagan: An Alternative Guide to Health & Well-being*

*Earth Spirit: Honoring the Wild – Reclaiming Witchcraft & Environmental Activism*
*Earth Spirit: Gaia, Saving Her, Saving Ourselves*

You may also like

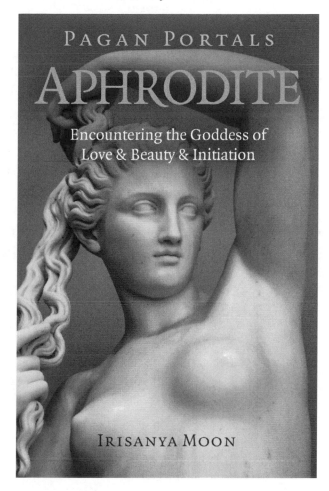

PAGAN PORTALS

APHRODITE

Encountering the Goddess of
Love & Beauty & Initiation

IRISANYA MOON

**Aphrodite**
*Encountering the Goddess of Love*
*& Beauty & Initiation*

Irisanya Moon

978-1-78904-347-1 (Paperback)
978-1-78904-348-8 (e-book)

## MOON BOOKS
### PAGANISM & SHAMANISM

What is Paganism? A religion, a spirituality, an alternative belief system, nature worship? You can fi nd support for all these definitions (and many more) in dictionaries, encyclopaedias, and text books of religion, but subscribe to any one and the truth will evade you. Above all Paganism is a creative pursuit, an encounter with reality, an exploration of meaning and an expression of the soul. Druids, Heathens, Wiccans and others, all contribute their insights and literary riches to the Pagan tradition. Moon Books invites you to begin or to deepen your own encounter, right here, right now.

If you have enjoyed this book, why not tell other readers by posting a review on your preferred book site.

Readers of ebooks can buy or view any of these bestsellers by clicking on the live link in the title. Most titles are published in paperback and as an ebook. Paperbacks are available in traditional bookshops. Both print and ebook formats are available online.

Find more titles and sign up to our readers' newsletter
http://www.johnhuntpublishing.com/paganism

For video content, author interviews and more, please subscribe to our YouTube channel.

## MoonBooksPublishing

Follow us on social media for book news, promotions and more:

## Facebook: Moon Books Publishing

## Instagram: @moonbooksjhp

## Twitter: @MoonBooksJHP

## Tik Tok: @moonbooksjhp